OCEANS APART

WHEN TWO WORLDS COLLIDE

- Book One: OCEANS APART
- Book Two: AGAINST ALL ODDS

OCEANS APART

When Love Crossed the Sea

Matthew Warburton

As seen on Channel 4's Nevermets

COPYRIGHT

WHEN TWO WORLDS COLLIDE — Book One: OCEANS APART
When Love Crossed the Sea
Copyright © 2026 by Matthew Warburton

This is a work of nonfiction.
Some names and identifying details may have been changed to protect privacy.

ISBN: 978-1-0369-6183-1
Series Title: When Two Worlds Collide
Cover Photo: Maria Gajo
Cover Design: Matthew Warburton
Edited by the author
Published by: Mattandmariavlog
Printed in the United Kingdom.

For permissions, inquiries, or rights requests, contact:
mattywarb@gmail.com

DEDICATION

For Maria —
the woman who turned a quiet life into a story worth telling.

For the girl who messaged me when I least expected it,
who stayed when distance tried to pull us apart,
who believed in us long before I believed in myself.

For the woman who taught me that love isn't found —
it's built, protected, fought for, and chosen every single day.

For every late-night call, every shared dream,
every moment you held me together from thousands of miles away.
For the laughter that carried me through the hardest days,
and the courage you gave me when I had none of my own.

For the way you saw me —
not as the man I was,
but as the man I could become.

For your patience, your strength, your softness,
and the way you loved me without conditions,
even when life made it difficult,
even when the world said no,
even when everything felt impossible.

This book exists because you existed in my life.

Because you changed the direction of my story.
Because you showed me what it means to fight for something real.

Everything I wrote here —
every memory, every truth, every moment —
is a testament to the love that survived distance,
defied circumstances,
and became the foundation of the life we're building now.

This book is for you, Maria.
My wife, my partner, my miracle.
The beginning, the middle, and the reason I kept going.

My reason, my courage, my everything.

"Some people fall in love across a room.
We fell in love across an ocean."

ACKNOWLEDGEMENTS

There are moments in life when you realize you didn't walk the road alone — even when it felt like you did. This book is the proof of that.

To my family, who stood beside me through every quiet struggle and every loud victory. Thank you for believing in me long before I believed in myself, and for welcoming Maria into your hearts with the same warmth you've always given me.

To Maria's family, who trusted me with their daughter from thousands of miles away. Your kindness, acceptance, and love made me feel like I had gained a second home long before I ever stepped foot in the Philippines.

To the friends who listened, encouraged, and reminded me that love was worth fighting for — even when the world made it difficult.

To the people who followed our journey on Channel 4's *Nevermets*, and to everyone who reached out on TikTok and YouTube — your messages, encouragement, and support meant the world. You helped us feel seen, believed, and celebrated every step of the way.

And finally, to Maria — my wife, my partner, my miracle. Thank you for your patience, your strength, your laughter, and your unwavering belief in us. You turned my life into something bigger, brighter, and braver than I ever imagined. This book exists because you existed in my life.

AUTHOR'S NOTE

This is not a story about perfection. It's a story about two people who tried — again and again —
even when distance, fear, and circumstance made everything harder than it needed to be.

Our story was followed on Channel 4's Nevermets, where viewers witnessed the highs and lows
of a long-distance relationship. This book tells the full story behind those moments:
the waiting, the planning, the heartbreak, and the love that carried us across oceans.

Some memories in these pages are beautiful. Some are painful. All of them are true.

If you're reading this because you've loved someone far away, I hope you see yourself in these pages.
If you're reading this because you're curious, I hope you understand the courage it takes to love across oceans.
And if you're reading this because you believe in love — real love — then I hope our story reminds you that distance doesn't break something meant to last.

This is where our journey began. But it's not where it ends.

— Matthew

CONTENTS

FOREWORD

I've known Matthew long enough to say this with certainty: he never does anything halfway. When he loves, he loves fully. When he commits, he commits with his whole heart. And when life handed him a love story separated by oceans, he didn't walk away — he walked toward it.

I watched this journey unfold from the outside, but close enough to feel its weight. I saw the late-night messages, the early-morning calls, the months of waiting, the hope, the fear, and the quiet determination that kept him going. What began as a simple connection became something deeper, something that reshaped him in ways he never expected.

This book is more than a memoir. It's a testament to patience, courage, and the kind of love that refuses to be defeated by distance. Matthew didn't just cross an ocean — he crossed every doubt he ever had about himself. And in doing so, he found not only the woman he loved, but the man he was always meant to become.

I'm proud of him for writing this.
And I'm proud of the life he built because of it.

—Angela Warburton

PREFACE

I never imagined I would write a book. For most of my life, I didn't think my story mattered enough to put on a page. But everything changed the day a message arrived from someone on the other side of the world — a message that would become the beginning of everything.

This memoir started as a way to remember. To hold on to the moments that shaped me, the conversations that carried me, and the love that grew stronger with every mile between us. I wanted to capture the truth of it — the loneliness before it all began, the hope that slowly returned, the fear of losing something I had barely found, and the courage it took to keep going.

I wrote this book because I wanted to honour the journey.
I wrote it because love like this deserves to be remembered.
And I wrote it because someone out there might need to know that distance doesn't make love impossible — it makes it extraordinary.

— Matthew Warburton

INTRODUCTION

Before this story begins, I want to tell you something honestly: nothing about this journey was easy. Not the waiting, not the distance, not the months of uncertainty. But every moment — even the hardest ones — led to something I never expected to find.

This book follows the path from the very beginning: the quiet years before the message, the first spark of connection, the long nights of video calls, the fear of losing hope, the planning, the delays, the heartbreak, and finally, the moment two people who had only ever known each other through screens stood face to face for the first time.

It's a story about love, yes — but also about healing, growth, and the bravery it takes to choose someone who lives a world away. It's about the small moments that become lifelines, the big moments that change everything, and the quiet moments that remind us why we hold on.

This is the story of how two hearts, separated by oceans, found their way to the same place.

And this is where it begins.

MASTER TIMELINE

2019 — The Beginning

- Matthew and Maria match online
- First messages
- First video call
- Relationship begins

2020 — Building a Long-Distance Life

- Daily calls become routine
- **March:** COVID lockdown begins
- WiFi issues create long stretches without video
- Emotional resilience grows
- **October:** One-year anniversary scrapbook
- Buying engagement ring
- **December:** Matt's family gets COVID
- "Saving Christmas" video

2021 — The Slow Return of Hope

- **January:** Matt gets COVID
- **February:** Vaccination
- Restrictions begin easing
- December 2021 meeting becomes possible

2021 — Delays, Distance, and Breakthroughs

- **Sept–Nov:** Maria's flights cancelled
- Maria returns home
- YouTube channel monetized
- Jan–Mar 2022: Channel earns £1,200
- Bird at hotel window moment
- Christmas week: 24/7 video calls
- Dumaguete hotel stay

2022 — Calm, Connection, and the First Message

- Early 2022: Maria settles back home
- Daily video calls return
- Beach walks, Turtle Island, Danjugan Island
- December 2022 becomes the new meeting plan
- Casting team discovers Matt's comment
- Casting message arrives
- First interview
- Engagement ring shown
- Programme sees relationship is genuine

2022 — The Months Between

- **March–July:** No confirmation
- Follow-up questions
- Growing certainty
- **July:** Joint Skype call

2022 — The Decision

- Joint call
- Officially selected
- Chosen as main couple
- Travel and filming prep begins

2022 — The Final Preparations

- Buying clothes for tropical heat
- Choosing travel gear
- Gathering years of gifts
- Waiting for passport
- Emotional conversations
- Packing
- Countdown becomes real

2022 — The Morning of the Trip

- Waking before the alarm
- Emotional goodbye with pets
- Final checks
- Sunrise departure

2022 — The Airport

- Security panic over the ring
- Waiting at the gate
- Boarding the plane

2022 — The Flight

- Window-seat reflections
- Spiritual feeling of travelling toward her
- Layover realisation
- Final descent

2022 — Arrival

- Manila arrival
- Terminal transfer
- Domestic flight to Bacolod
- Emotional night in hotel
- Bus to Sipalay
- The moment she said "Babe"

2022 — The Hug That Changed Everything

- Emotional collision
- First hug
- First kiss
- Crowd cheering
- Van ride together

2022 — Our Little Yellow House

- Tricycle ride
- Arriving at the yellow house
- Meeting her parents

- First walk to the beach
- Kids giggling
- Crew dismissing them for the night
- First evening alone

2022 — Our First Morning Together

- Waking up together
- Breakfast on the porch
- Becoming part of the neighbourhood

2022 — Sipalay Market, Pearl Beach & The First Proposal

- Trip to Sipalay market
- Sunset grilling at Pearl Beach
- Honest conversation about the future
- First proposal (private, incomplete)

2022 — The Awkward Day, The Announcement & The Midnight Meeting

- Morning tension
- Mountain hike
- Sister's farewell party
- Engagement announcement
- Midnight walk
- Private apology to her father
- Father's acceptance

2022 — The Blessing & The Journey to Danjugan Island

- Official blessing
- Tropical rainstorm
- Boat to Danjugan
- Island tour
- Snorkeling with turtles
- Cliff-edge lookout

2022 — The Real Proposal

- Candlelit dinner
- Taking the ring back
- Kneeling properly
- Maria's emotional yes
- Fireflies surrounding the hammock

2022 — The Last Morning, The Goodbye & The Journey Home

- Final morning on Danjugan
- Gifts
- Official engagement announcement
- Final hour in the yellow house
- Emotional goodbye
- Bus to Bacolod
- Flight to Manila
- Flight to London

Epilogue — The Beginning After the Beginning

- Landing in London
- Emotional shift from hope to belief
- Returning to long-distance life
- Renewed determination
- Understanding this is only the beginning

PRELUDE

The Moment Before Everything

There are moments in life that don't feel real when you're standing inside them.
 Moments that feel suspended, weightless, as if time itself is holding its breath.
 Moments that don't announce themselves as important — they simply arrive, quiet and unassuming, and wait for you to notice.

I didn't know it then — not fully — but I was standing in one of those moments.

Not at the beginning.
 Not at the end.
 Somewhere in between.

A place where the past and the future touched for the first time, so softly that I almost missed it.

I remember the glow of my phone screen in the dark, the quiet hum of a world that had no idea what was about to happen. The room around me was still — the kind of stillness that feels almost sacred, like the universe was clearing its throat before speaking.
 I remember the weight of the day on my shoulders, the familiar heaviness of routine, and the strange sense that something in the air felt different, even if I couldn't name it.

It wasn't dramatic.
It wasn't loud.
It wasn't the kind of moment you'd point to and say, "That's when everything changed."

But it was.

I remember lying there, half-awake, half-lonely, scrolling through my phone the way people do when they're searching for something but don't know what it is. The light from the screen painted the room in soft blue shadows, catching the edges of things — the bedside table, the curtains, the tired lines on my hands.
It was a familiar scene, one I'd lived a hundred times before.

And yet… something felt different.

There was a quietness inside me that didn't feel empty.
A stillness that didn't feel numb.
A sense — faint, fragile — that something was shifting beneath the surface.

I didn't know what it meant.
I didn't know what it would become.
I didn't know that a single moment, a single choice, a single message could alter the trajectory of a life.

But I felt it.
A pull.
A spark.
A whisper in the chest said: **Pay attention.**

Because sometimes the universe doesn't shout.
 Sometimes it doesn't send signs, storms, or revelations.
 Sometimes it sends a single moment — small, fragile, easy to overlook —
and trusts you to step into it.

I didn't know that I was only one message away from everything
changing.
 I didn't know that the smile I would soon see on a screen would become a
home.
 I didn't know that a stranger 7,000 miles away would become the centre
of my world.

All I knew was that something in me was shifting.
 Quietly.
Gently.
 Like the first ripple on still water.

If I had known what that moment would lead to —
 the joy, the distance, the ache, the miracles, the airports, the storms, the
rings, the goodbyes, the beginnings —
 I don't know if I would have believed it.

But I would have stepped into it anyway.

Because some stories don't wait for you to be ready.
 Some stories begin the moment your heart whispers yes, even if your
mind hasn't caught up.

And that night — that quiet, ordinary night — my heart whispered
something I didn't yet understand.

This is the moment before everything.
The breath before the first word.
The spark before the flame.
The quiet before the message that changed my life.

And if I close my eyes, I can still feel it —
that soft, impossible shift in the air,
the night my world began to rewrite itself.

A moment so small it could have passed unnoticed.
A moment so gentle it could have slipped through my fingers.
A moment that didn't look like a beginning at all.

But it was.

It was the doorway.
The threshold.
The first step onto a path I didn't know I was already walking.

And the truth is — the story didn't begin with the message.
It began with the feeling.
The quiet ache.
The longing I tried to ignore.
The sense that something in my life was unfinished, waiting, incomplete.

Before the message, there was emptiness.
Before the connection, there was loneliness.
Before Maria, there was the drifting.

And that's where the story truly starts.

Not with the moment I pressed send.

Not with the moment she replied.

But with the life I was living before I ever knew her name.

The life that made me ready — even when I didn't know I was.

The life that shaped the man who would fall in love with a stranger across an ocean.

The life that brought me to the edge of everything I didn't know I was waiting for.

And so, before the message...

before the first hello...

before the first call...

before the first moment I realised I was falling...

There was a beginning I didn't recognise.

A beginning that looked like nothing at all.

A beginning that felt like just another night.

A beginning that would lead me to her.

And that is where the story continues.

PROLOGUE

Before the Beginning

Before the flights, before the island, before the moment I finally held her in my arms, there was only a screen — a small glowing window connecting two people who had no idea how much their lives were about to change.

It didn't feel like a beginning.
Not then.
Not in the quiet of that night when everything still looked ordinary.

But beginnings rarely look like beginnings when you're living them.

It started with a message I almost didn't send.
A simple thought, a small impulse, the kind you usually ignore.
Nothing dramatic.
Nothing that announced itself as fate.

Just a name I didn't recognise.
A profile I'd scrolled past before.
A moment so small it could have slipped past unnoticed.

But it didn't.
Something in me paused.
Something in me reached out.

Maybe it was curiosity.

Maybe it was loneliness.
Maybe it was the quiet ache I'd been carrying for longer than I wanted to admit.

Or maybe — and I believe this now — it was the echo of the moment I'd felt earlier, that soft shift in the air, the whisper that something was coming.

I didn't know that this message would become the thread that pulled me across an ocean.
I didn't know it would lead to airports and promises, heartbreak and hope, distance and devotion.
I didn't know it would lead me to her.

All I knew was that I typed the words.
Simple ones.
Small ones.
The kind you send without expecting anything back.

But sometimes the smallest choices are the ones that change everything.

And that night — the night after the moment before everything — I pressed send.

That's where the story truly begins.

CHAPTER ONE

BEFORE THE MESSAGE

Growing up, I felt depressed and alone. School was a dark time for me — I didn't fit in, I didn't have friends, and I didn't know how to change any of it. I felt invisible most days, like I was just passing through the halls unnoticed. It was a lonely way to grow up, and it left a mark that followed me into adulthood.

By fourteen, something finally shifted. Bowling entered my life at exactly the moment I needed it. Being on a team with my grandad, practicing with my nan and grandad every weekend — it gave me a purpose, a routine, a place where I wasn't invisible. If I hadn't had that, I honestly don't know who or what I would have turned into. It's scary to think about the path I could have gone down.

Bowling didn't just give me a hobby — it brought me closer to my grandparents than I had ever been before. It gave me something to hold onto when everything else felt empty.

And it didn't just bring me closer to them — it brought me closer to my whole family at home too. Two years after I started, my dad joined the league and ended up playing on my team. A year later, my mum began coming along as well — not to bowl, but to watch, to support, to be part of it.

On Sundays, I played doubles with my nan, and my mum even became the captain of our team. For the first time in my life, we weren't just a family living under the same roof — we were a family doing something together. Bowling became our weekly ritual, the one place where we all showed up for each other.

Years later, something happened in my family — sudden, heartbreaking, and completely unexpected — and it shook me awake. It made me look at my own life in a way I never had before. I realised how isolated I was, how stuck I felt, how little I was actually living. I remember thinking that I had family who loved me, but no friends, no social life, no real future unless I changed something. It was a moment that forced me to confront the truth: if I didn't take control of my life, nothing was ever going to change.

That moment became the catalyst.
 The turning point.
 The push I didn't want, but desperately needed.

I knew I could never harm myself — that wasn't in me — but I also knew I couldn't keep living the way I was. I wanted more. I needed more. I wanted a relationship, a partner, a family, a life that meant something. I wanted love. I wanted to be seen. I wanted to be chosen.

But as I got older and work took over, even bowling started slipping away. Working the 2–10 shift drained me completely. It made me depressed, anxious, and exhausted. I couldn't make it to all the matches anymore. Weeknight games started at seven, so I had to use my holidays just to attend. Bowling stopped feeling like a joy and started feeling like something I was fighting to keep alive. Little by little, I lost interest. Not because I didn't love it, but because life had worn me down.

Every night was the same. I'd come home from the 2–10 shift, go straight to my room, and eat alone with only my dog Milo for company. He was always excited to see me, always waiting, always ready to sit beside me like he understood everything I wasn't saying. Without him, those nights would have been truly empty.

I filled my time with movies and games — most of my money went on them — and I'd scroll through my phone or sit at my desktop watching YouTube for hours. I didn't talk to anyone. I hadn't had friends in a very long time. I had coworkers, but not people who checked in on me, not people who cared. The silence was heavy. I felt isolated, like my room was my only escape from the outside world. My nights felt empty because my entire existence felt empty.

Sometimes I went out with people from work when they went to the club at the weekend. I tried to enjoy it, but I never really did. I wasn't the loud one, or the confident one, or the one who could walk up to someone and start talking. I always ended up in the same place — sitting in the corner, nursing a drink, watching everyone else live the life I wished I had. I didn't want to be alone. I just wanted someone to be there with me.

By early 2019, something inside me shifted again. I can't pinpoint the exact day, but I knew my life was passing me by. I felt empty, lost, and unlovable — like nobody was ever going to choose me. And the hardest part was knowing that nothing was going to change unless I changed it myself. Nobody was offering me anything. Nobody was knocking on my door with a chance at love. If I wanted something different, I had to take a step.

I used to tell myself I wasn't looking for a movie moment. I'd watched a million films where the dorky guy somehow ends up with the beautiful girl, and I always thought, "That's not real life. That doesn't happen to people like me."

But deep down, I think I was looking for it. Not the Hollywood version — just the feeling of being chosen. The feeling of someone seeing me, wanting me, picking me out of the crowd.

So I joined the dating sites. I didn't know what I was looking for or if anything would come of it. I just wanted one real connection — someone to notice me, even for a few seconds. Someone who might look at me and think I was worth talking to. That was everything.

Before I ever downloaded a dating app, my mindset was strange — a mix of hope and disbelief. I was ready for change, desperate for it even, but I didn't truly believe it would happen for me. Still, I was willing to try. I was curious. I was hopeful that maybe, at the very least, I'd find someone to chat with. Someone who might help me build a bit of confidence. Someone who might change the way I saw myself and the world.

I hoped somebody would notice me. I knew I shouldn't just message the first beautiful girls I saw — but of course, that's exactly what I did anyway. I have good taste, after all.

The first girl I messaged hadn't been online for months, but she eventually found me later on. We were actually preparing to meet — she was a local girl with children. When she didn't message back, I moved on to the next beautiful girl, the Chinese girl who lived only twenty miles away. I hadn't expected either of them to reply, never mind wanting to meet me in person, but they both did. The Chinese girl even gave me her number right away because we both agreed the dating site felt creepy. It felt strange — almost unreal — that girls like that were responding to me. And in that moment, something inside me shifted. I started to believe that maybe I could find love this way. Maybe I could find a connection.

Then there was the Filipina. We only talked for a few hours — nothing deep, nothing serious. She disappeared quickly because she was scared of committing to anything. It wasn't a connection — just another reminder that I wanted someone who wouldn't run at the first sign of something real.

I even went on a date before sorting my debt. I liked her, but afterwards I realised something important: if I wanted a real relationship, I needed to get my life in order. I couldn't offer anything while I was £13,000 in debt. So I went to StepChange, made a plan, and started fixing things. It wasn't dramatic. It was just a quiet decision to be better for whoever might come next.

More than anything, I wanted a conversation that lasted more than a day. I wanted to be someone's reason to come back and talk again. I wanted someone real — someone who wouldn't disappear, someone who would see me for who I really was and give me the time to become the person I knew I could be. That's why I turned to the apps. Because when I'm texting, I can express my thoughts and feelings in a way I never could face-to-face. Texting gave me a chance to build something slowly, honestly, and safely. Building a connection was always the long-term plan.

Each girl taught me something.
 Each almost-connection shaped me.
 Each disappointment pushed me closer to the truth.

I wasn't looking for perfection.
 I wasn't looking for a fantasy or a Hollywood moment.
 I was looking for someone real.
 Someone consistent.
 Someone who wanted me back.

And without realising it, all of these false starts were preparing me for the moment that would change everything.

The moment Maria replied.

Even when I went to the club with people from work, it didn't feel like I belonged. I wasn't alone the whole night — I'd arrived with a group of coworkers, mostly couples, and in truth it was just a chance to get out of the house. That was the whole reason I went. I knew I needed to break the routine of work, home, silence, repeat. But even surrounded by ten or more people, it still felt like I was on my own. There were moments where it felt like I had friends, and then moments where I felt completely alone, even though we were all standing right there together.

I'd sit in the corner and wish someone would notice me, but deep down I knew they wouldn't. I had felt low for most of my life. Self-confidence wasn't something I had — not even a little. I felt invisible to the whole world, even in a crowded club with music blasting and people laughing around me. And yes, I was embarrassed. I knew I looked like I was sulking, sitting there on my own, but I couldn't change it. I felt out of place, like I didn't fit into the world everyone else seemed to move through so easily.

By the time I reached the end of all those almost-connections, I was tired. Not just physically — emotionally. I tried. I've learned. I'd put myself out there more than I ever had in my life. And still, nothing had stuck. Nothing had turned into anything real.

There were nights I lay in bed staring at the ceiling, wondering if I was fooling myself — if I was meant to stay alone forever, if I was asking for too much. Just wanting someone to talk to, someone to care, someone to choose me.

There was a point where I genuinely thought about deleting everything. The apps, the profiles, the conversations. I felt like maybe love just wasn't meant for me. Maybe I'd missed my chance. Maybe I was too late. Maybe I was too broken. Maybe I was just meant to stay in my room forever, watching life happen to other people.

But something in me refused to give up.
A tiny voice — quiet, but stubborn — kept saying:
"Try one more time."

Not because I was confident.
Not because I believed something magical would happen.
Not because I thought I deserved anything special.

But because I wasn't ready to go back to the life I had been living.
I wasn't ready to return to the silence.
I wasn't ready to accept that loneliness was all I'd ever know.

So I opened the apps again.
 I refreshed the screen.
 I took a breath.

I wasn't looking for perfection.
 I wasn't looking for fireworks.
 I wasn't even looking for love.

I was looking for a spark — the smallest sign that someone, somewhere,
might see me.

And then it happened.
 A new match.
 A new name.
 A new face.
 A message that would change everything.

I didn't know it then — how could I? — but I was standing on the edge of
the biggest moment of my life. The moment where everything I'd lived
through, everything I'd struggled with, everything I'd hoped for... finally
led somewhere.

The moment before Maria.

Looking back now, it's strange to think how close I came to giving up
right before everything changed. I didn't know it then — how could I? —
but all the loneliness, all the almost-connections, all the nights wondering
if I'd ever be chosen... they were leading me to a single moment. A
moment so small it barely felt real at first. A notification. A name. A
message. The quiet beginning of the life I'd been waiting for.

CHAPTER TWO

TWO HEARTS, TWO COUNTRIES

I didn't expect anything to come from that first message.

It was late — the kind of late where the house is quiet, the world feels small, and your thoughts feel louder than they should. The kind of late where you scroll not because you're looking for anything, but because you're trying to fill a silence you've grown too used to.

I was lying in bed, the room dim except for the glow of my phone, scrolling through my feed with half-interest, half-habit. I wasn't searching for love. I wasn't searching for anything, really. I was just passing time, trying to quiet the restless feeling in my chest that had been there for months — maybe years.

And honestly, I was close to giving up.

I'd spoken to other girls, and for a moment it felt like something might happen — but nothing ever went anywhere. My heart was tired of false starts. Tired of almosts. Tired of waiting for something real.

I guess my heart couldn't wait anymore. It saw Maria and said yes before my brain even caught up.

And then I saw her.

A smile that felt warm even through a screen.
 Eyes that seemed to hold a story — not loud, not dramatic, but deep.
 Something about her drew me in instantly.

Not her bio.
 Not her details.
 Not anything written.

Just her.

And something about her was different.

I'd never felt that moment — that spark — with anyone before. I couldn't
stop looking at her smile and her big, beautiful eyes. She looked so sweet,
so gentle, so real.

She looked like the girl I'd been waiting for my whole life.

When I looked at her photo, it felt like her eyes were speaking to me —
like there was something there, something real, something worth taking a
chance on.

I hesitated.

My thumb hovered over the message box. My hands were shaking. My
chest felt tight. Time felt like it had slowed down. Before I even realised it,
I'd sat up in bed, smiling like an idiot.

I almost talked myself out of it — the way I had so many times before.

She won't reply.
 She's probably not even real.

What's the point?
Why risk another silence?

But something — something small, something stubborn, something tired of being cautious — pushed me forward.

I typed a simple message:

"Hi, how are you?"

I pressed send.

And in that tiny moment — that click, that heartbeat — my life shifted, even though I didn't feel it yet.

Her reply came quicker than I expected:

"Hello! I'm good, thank you. How about you?"

Her message felt warm, friendly, open — not forced, not cold, not distant. There was something in her tone, even through text, that felt genuine.

I typed back.

And before I knew it, we were talking.

Not small talk — real talk. The kind that flows easily, like two people who were meant to find each other without even knowing it.

A few messages in, she asked:

"Where are you from?"

"England," I typed. "Warrington."

"Oh wow… that's far," she replied.

I smiled at my phone.

"I know. What about you?"

There was a pause — a longer one this time — and then she replied:

"I'm Filipina."

I blinked. I hadn't known. I hadn't read her bio. I hadn't looked at anything except her smile — and somehow, that had been enough.

Before I could respond, another message appeared:

"But I'm working abroad right now."

"Abroad?" I typed. "Where?"

"In the UAE," she said. "For two years."

I sat up a little straighter.

Two years. Two countries. Two lives that had never crossed before.

But instead of pulling away, something in me leaned closer — like a magnet I didn't realise was there.

I stared at her photo again — the warmth in her smile, the softness in her eyes — and something inside me pushed forward before my brain could stop it.

"You are really beautiful," I typed. "I really like you."

The moment I pressed send, my heart dropped into my stomach.

It felt bold. Too bold. Too honest for someone I'd just met.

The typing dots appeared... disappeared... appeared again.

Then her message came through:

"I like you too... but I'm too far away. How can we do this?"

My heart was pounding.

I wasn't calm. I wasn't smooth. I wasn't confident. I was nervous —
properly nervous — but I knew I had to be honest.

Because the truth was, I'd latched onto her instantly.

I could tell she was real with me — not fake, not playing games. There was
something in her energy, her honesty. I couldn't explain it, but I trusted it.

So I typed, slowly, carefully:

"I know it sounds crazy...

but I'll save.
 We'll talk every day.
 We'll video call.
 We'll get to know each other properly.
 And when you go back home to the Philippines...

I'll come to you."

I stared at the message before sending it.

My thumb hovered.

My stomach twisted.

But I pressed send anyway.

Because I meant it.
Because I didn't want to lose her.
Because I didn't want to be "just chat mates."
Because I wanted her — really wanted her — to be my girlfriend.

The typing dots appeared... disappeared... appeared again.

Then she sent the message that stopped my breath:

"You would really come to the Philippines for me?"

I swallowed hard and typed back:

"Yes. I will. I want this... I want you."

There was a long pause — the kind that feels like the whole world is holding its breath.

Then she typed:

"Okay... let's try."

And that was it.

Not "maybe."
Not "let's see."
Not "just chatting."

That was the moment we became something real.

A real plan.
A real commitment.
A real beginning.

And when she said "let's try," everything in me lit up.

I reread her message over and over, almost in disbelief — but deep down, I knew.

This moment had just changed my life.

Two hearts.
Two countries.
One decision — made on day one.

From the outside, it was just two strangers messaging on their phones.

But inside, something was shifting — two worlds slowly leaning toward each other.

I didn't know it yet, but this was the start of a story that would carry us through years of distance, lockdowns, heartbreak, laughter, and moments that felt impossible.

A story that would cross oceans.

A story that would bring her into my life, my home, my world.

A story that began with a message... and grew into something real.

As the hours passed, the conversation deepened.

We talked about food, family, work, dreams, fears, music.

She told me she loved Westlife.

"I grew up listening to them too," I said.

"Really?" she replied.

"Really."

She told me about her family back home, how she missed them, how she worked abroad to support them.

I told her about my quiet routines, my job, my family, and my dog Milo.

She laughed at my jokes — even the bad ones.

I laughed at her teasing — especially when she called me shy.

The conversation didn't last long — she had been messaging just before going to sleep. I'd caught her at the end of her day.

We talked just long enough to exchange numbers and move to WhatsApp. She said we could talk more in the morning.

Before she logged off, she said softly:

"Goodnight, Matt."

"Goodnight, Maria."

When the chat ended, I sat there staring at the screen, feeling something I hadn't felt in a long time.

Hope.

Not the loud, dramatic kind.

The quiet kind — the kind that settles in your chest without asking.

And somewhere between the messages, the laughter, and the honesty...

I realised something had shifted.

I didn't feel as alone.

She was thousands of miles away.

But somehow, she felt closer than anyone else in my life.

I didn't tell anyone about her.

It felt like our secret — something fragile, something real, something I didn't want the world touching yet.

I barely slept that night.

I kept rereading our messages. Looking at her photos — she'd sent a few more on WhatsApp.

She looked amazing.

I couldn't believe someone like her was talking to someone like me.

Two hearts.
 Two countries.
 One beginning.

I didn't sleep much that night.

And when morning came, everything changed again — because that was the day I heard her voice for the very first time.

CHAPTER THREE

THE FIRST VIDEO CALL

Where reality replaces imagination, and everything becomes real.

Before the call, we were texting — the kind where everything feels easier because you're not saying it out loud. We were leaning into something without fully admitting it yet. It felt safe. Controlled. You could think before you spoke.

She was on her break, getting ready to go back to work. I was lying there, replying, caught in that strange mix of excitement and disbelief that someone like her was talking to someone like me.

Then she asked:

"Can I see you?"

Everything in my head just... stopped.

Not because I didn't want to — but because the idea of seeing her, properly seeing her, felt unreal. I'd been staring at her photos, imagining her smile, replaying it in my head.

And now that imagination was about to become real.

She wanted to make sure I was real.

Truth is... I wanted the same.

When the call came through, I froze.

Completely.

Then I answered.

And the second her face appeared, I smiled without even thinking about it.

She was naturally beautiful — not in a posed, filtered way, but real. Soft. Warm. The kind of beauty that hits you because it's genuine.

And it didn't make sense to me.

This girl — this sweet, stunning girl — was calling me. Wanting to see me.

That alone felt unreal.

We'd added each other on Facebook that morning, so the first few minutes were her trying to find me there. It was clumsy, a bit chaotic, but easy. The kind of moment that already feels like a shared joke.

Then the video call settled.

And my confidence disappeared.

I've never been the guy who video calls girls like her.
 I've never been the guy they want to see.

So when it became real, I didn't know what to do.

"Hi," she said.

"Hi," I replied.

And then... nothing.

Panic.

Instead of speaking, I started typing.

On a video call.

It was ridiculous — but I couldn't stop myself.

"I'm shy," I typed.

She laughed.

Not at me — just softly, naturally, like it didn't bother her at all.

That helped.

So I typed again:

"You're so beautiful."
 "I love your eyes."

She smiled — properly smiled this time — and it hit differently seeing it live, not frozen in a photo.

"Why are you so shy?" she asked.

And this time, I answered honestly:

"Because I really like you."

There was a pause after that.

Not awkward — just... real.

That moment changed something.

She wasn't laughing at me.

If anything, she liked it.

The call didn't last long.

I didn't have the confidence to carry it, and everything still felt overwhelming — like my brain was trying to catch up with what was happening in real time.

But it didn't matter.

Because it was real.

We ended the call and went straight back to texting.

Then she said something that stuck with me:

"Soon you won't be so shy."

That line meant more than she probably realised.

It meant she wasn't put off.
 It meant she wanted to keep going.
 It meant she saw something worth staying for.

And for me, that was everything.

She went back to work.

I got ready for mine.

But the conversation didn't stop.

We texted while I got in the bath, while I got dressed, while I sat in the car — even walking into work.

It already felt natural. Like we'd slipped into each other's routine without even trying.

After that call, something shifted.

This wasn't just curiosity anymore.

This wasn't just hope.

This felt real.

I was falling for her.

Honestly... I think I already had.

I'd never experienced anything like it — someone so kind, so warm, so genuinely interested in me.

She told me I was cute.
 She told me I was handsome.

I didn't know how to process that.

I've never seen myself that way, so hearing it from her felt strange... but also good. Like something inside me was starting to change.

We talked about our height difference — me at 6'3", her at 5'1".

We laughed about it.

She said she liked that I was tall.

It was a small thing, but it stayed with me.

Because it made me feel seen.

And in the quiet moments after the call, one thing became clear:

She felt it too.

There was something real building between us.

Two hearts.
 Two countries.
 One connection — no longer just an idea.

Looking back now, that first video call wasn't perfect.

It was awkward.
 Short.
 Unpolished.

But it was honest.

It was the moment everything changed — from imagination to reality.

For the first time, this wasn't just something happening on a screen.

It was happening to me.

And the most important part?

She saw me.

Not a filtered version.
 Not a confident version.

The real me — shy, unsure, figuring it out as I went.

And she stayed.

That was the moment I should have realised:

This was different.

Because soon, I'd learn what it really meant to miss someone...

Even before they were gone.

CHAPTER FOUR

BUILDING A LIFE FROM A DISTANCE

You don't always notice the moment a routine becomes a relationship. It doesn't arrive with fireworks or announcements. It slips in quietly — in the way someone stays on video call with you while you get ready for work, or the way you start smiling at your phone without realizing it. That was November 2019 for us. The month everything shifted from "talking" to something real.

We had already been together privately for over a month, and we had talked about many things during that time — like changing our Facebook status to "In a relationship." We had waited many weeks since deciding this, but waited a little while longer. We wanted it to feel right, not rushed.

When we finally did it — that morning in November — it felt huge. I walked into work with a smile I couldn't hide. Everyone at work could see it. My mum had already noticed I'd been smiling more, texting almost nonstop, disappearing into my room more. She knew something was happening, but she didn't know what.

By then, our routine had already formed. It became our thing: video calls and texting. We stayed on video call but often typed instead of talking. It sounded strange to everyone else, but it was perfect. She stayed with me until she had to leave for work, sometimes ending the call only when absolutely necessary. Sometimes it was just us — intimate in a way that didn't need words.

At night, she stayed awake until I fell asleep. We'd video call again. She'd fall asleep with me watching her. I'd see glimpses of her sleeping, peaceful and soft, and something in me settled. Sometimes I left the video call running, her sleeping on my screen while my phone sat in my locker for a few hours. If the connection lasted, I would take her "home" while she slept. Then it was my turn. I would fall asleep while watching her, and she would wake first and see me. I didn't know it then, but that was the beginning of love.

On November 2 — exactly one month since we first talked — we celebrated our first monthsary. Maria had suggested celebrating every month we were together. Birthdays don't come around very often, so why not keep something positive going? It felt small and huge at the same time. Those little milestones made the distance easier. They made us feel closer.

Around that time, we picked up little habits from other long-distance couples — like calling each other "babe." It wasn't planned. It just stuck.

My evenings had a rhythm. After work, I'd take Milo out for his walk, bringing Maria with me on video call. She came with me through the cold air, through familiar corners of my childhood. I showed her the little grassy patch where I played as a kid. I didn't realise it then, but I was letting her into my early life — the part of me that existed long before we met.

And then there was the cat.

A stray cat had started following me and Milo. Thin and cheeky, always a few steps behind us. Milo didn't mind; he just wanted to play. He even started asking to go to the patch at night because he knew the cat appeared there. Maria watched all of this on video call — laughing, reacting, becoming part of my world in the most ordinary, gentle way.

It took months before the cat trusted us enough to come inside. Eventually, he did. I brought him home to my mum's house, and he became her cat and Milo's friend. Looking back, those quiet nights — the dog, the cat, the patch, the calls — were the soft background of our early love story. Life was shifting, and I didn't even notice.

And then came the night she messaged my mum.

I went outside at 8 p.m. on my last break, expecting to chat with Maria as usual. She called me.

"I can't text... I'm texting Mum. She'll see our Facebook."

I froze. Then I laughed. Then I smiled so hard my face hurt.

She gave me that cheeky little smile... and then she turned off the call. I knew she was up to something. That sweet face, that smile, those big, beautiful eyes.

When I got home, my mum was waiting in the kitchen.

"Is there something you want to tell me?"

I froze, then smiled.

"Maybe," I said. "How much do you know?"

Then she said it:

"Somebody told me everything."

I showed her some pictures of Maria, grabbed a drink, and went up to my bedroom, heart racing. Maria video-called me and sent me the messages they had shared.

"Hi. I am Maria, Matt's girlfriend."

Who does that?
 Someone who feels the same as me.

That moment connected our worlds. Mum laughed, smiled, accepted her instantly, and realised this wasn't casual. She was proud of me. Proud of us. She wanted to be part of my life.

It was around this time that we said "I love you."

It wasn't dramatic. It wasn't planned. It just came out — natural, quiet, real.
 She said it first.
 And that was the moment everything changed.

Maria had explained early on that she was working a two-year contract that would end late September 2021. We discussed our first meeting. That gave me almost two years to save and plan for our future.

The future suddenly felt real. I confessed something I'd never admitted before: I'd never travelled alone — not even within the UK — and the idea of flying halfway around the world terrified me. But I would do anything to be with her.

Maria said she was okay traveling alone and would visit me first if needed. But a feeling of uneasiness lingered about her visiting the UK.

We explored the possibility of a UK visit visa but soon realised it wasn't feasible: strict requirements, high refusal rates, and the risk of affecting future applications. Completely off the table.

The plan changed. I would go to the Philippines once she returned from the UAE. We discussed timing and options, and the most sensible time was December 2021. My three-week holiday entitlement plus the Christmas break gave us a full 30 days together. Perfect.

We weren't just talking anymore — we were planning.
 This was our first real step into the future.

I asked her about the ring on her right hand. She said her cousin had given it to her. One night, I asked her to measure it.

"Why?" she asked.

I shrugged it off. Pretending it was nothing. I didn't tell her the truth. I was already thinking about an engagement ring. I needed the size. I needed to imagine asking her to marry me. She sent the measurements without realising why. One day she would understand.

Around the same time, we did something unusual for a new couple: researching visa rules. Maria told me that if it worked, she would come to the UK permanently. Not because she didn't love her home, but because I couldn't earn enough to live in the Philippines.

"The only way for us to be together is for me to come there," she said.

And she was right.

We sat thousands of miles apart, scrolling through the UK government website, reading requirements, timelines, trying to understand a system we didn't know we'd spend years navigating. Early, maybe — but it felt natural. We were already building something real.

December brought something Maria had never seen before: snow.

One evening it started falling in Warrington. Soft, quiet. During a video call, she could see it. I took her outside. She was so excited — like a kid seeing magic for the first time.

I built a small snowman for her, holding the phone so she could watch me shape it with freezing hands. She laughed at my cold fingers, I laughed at her laughter.

She'd never seen snow before — it's always hot in the Philippines. And there I was, standing outside in the cold, building a snowman for the woman I was falling in love with — while she was warm in the UAE and I couldn't feel my fingers.

Christmas came — our first Christmas as a couple. Long-distance, emotional, full of calls and messages. I showed her the tree in my mum's house once it was decorated.

Then New Year's Eve — counting down together on video call. Talking about the future. Feeling hopeful and connected.

By 2020, we weren't just in love.
 We were building a life.

CHAPTER FIVE

BUILDING A FUTURE

January arrived quietly — no fireworks, no drama — but something in our relationship shifted. We entered the new year not as two people trying to figure each other out, but as a couple — steady, comfortable, and sure.

The routines we built in those early weeks became the rhythm of our days. Morning calls. Break calls. Nightly calls. Falling asleep together. Waking up together. It all felt natural now. Effortless. Like breathing.

We talked more — about our days, our families, our routines, our fears, our hopes. The conversations weren't always deep or dramatic. Sometimes they were simple, everyday things. But that was the point. We were becoming part of each other's lives in a way that felt real and grounded.

Future planning became normal too. We talked more about December 2021, imagining what we'd do when we finally met. We talked about marriage in a soft, early way — not as a proposal, but as a dream. We talked about living together in the UK, about what life would look like, about how we'd make it work. Visa conversations came up again — lightly, without the weight they would eventually carry.

Around this time, we started watching LDR YouTube channels together — couples documenting their long-distance journeys, sharing struggles, reunions, tips, and stories. One night, we realised some of them were earning money from it. And just like that, we had an idea.

We created our own LDR YouTube channel.

It wasn't about fame or attention. It was about building something together. Something that could help her when she returned home to the Philippines. The plan was simple: I would earn money in the UK, the channel would grow, and whatever it made would go to her so she wouldn't have to work. It was our first shared project — our first attempt at building a future with our own hands.

February came, and Liverpool were dominating the Premier League. I talked about football more than she probably wanted to hear, but she listened anyway, smiling, pretending to understand it all. It became another thread in the fabric of our daily life.

February and March arrived with three important days:

— Valentine's Day on February 14

— Maria's birthday on March 4

— My birthday on March 21

Valentine's Day that year felt different — not because of distance, but because of the way she made it feel. In the days leading up to it, she kept smiling at her phone, hiding something from the camera. She told me she was drawing, but wouldn't let me see it. Every time I asked, she'd laugh, shake her head, and cover the page with her hand. I could see her excitement — the planning, the care, the way she wanted it to be a surprise.

I wanted to give her something too, something real even if I couldn't physically hand it to her. So I bought roses — proper red roses — and put them in water on the bathroom cupboard. When we video-called, I showed them to her. It wasn't the same as giving them in person — but it was the closest I could get. The way she smiled when she saw them made everything worth it.

When she finally showed me her gift, it was a personal note surrounded by flowers she had drawn herself. Simple. Thoughtful. Completely her. The way she smiled while showing it to me made the whole moment feel warm and real. Even through a screen, it felt like Valentine's Day.

We celebrated hers first — long-distance, but full of love. Birthdays in an LDR are strange. They make the distance feel sharper, the absence heavier. But they also make the love feel stronger somehow. I tried to make her feel special, and she did the same for me. Even through a screen, it mattered.

A few weeks later, it was my turn. She celebrated me the same way — calls, messages, small surprises. She made me feel seen and valued. And somehow, even through a screen, it was enough. Our birthdays became another reminder of how close we were, even with thousands of miles between us.

By mid-March, everything felt stable. We were happy. We were planning. We were dreaming. The future felt clear. Bright. Like something we could actually reach if we just kept going.

And then the news started.

A virus.
Cases rising.
Borders closing.
Uncertainty spreading faster than the illness itself.

We didn't know it yet, but everything was about to change.

CHAPTER SIX

COVID BEGINS (March 2020)

The month the world stopped — and the month we learned how much we meant to each other.

In the beginning, it didn't feel real. News headlines were just noise in the background — something happening far away — something that didn't belong to us. A virus in another country. A few cases here and there. People online arguing about whether it was serious or not. Life still felt normal enough that we didn't think twice about it.

But slowly, the tone of the world changed.

Shops started running out of essentials. People were panic-buying toilet rolls and pasta like the apocalypse was coming. Schools began closing. Offices sent people home. Every day, the news grew darker. Heavier. Closer.

And then one day, it wasn't "somewhere else" anymore.

It was here.

The UK announced a lockdown. Streets emptied overnight. The world outside my window went quiet — no cars, no kids playing, no normal life.

Just stillness. A strange, eerie stillness that didn't feel like peace. It felt like fear.

Inside the house, everything felt different too. My parents were worried. And I was trying to make sense of a world that suddenly made no sense at all.

But the biggest shift wasn't outside — it was between me and Maria.

Before COVID, our relationship had a rhythm. We talked every day, but life still had its own pace. Work, routines, errands, the normal distractions of everyday life. But when the world shut down, all of that disappeared. Suddenly, it was just us — two people in two different countries, trying to hold onto something real while everything else felt like it was falling apart.

Our conversations changed. They became longer, deeper, more emotional. We checked on each other constantly.

"Are you okay?"
"Are you safe?"
"Do you have food?"
"Are you scared?"

We were living the same crisis, but from opposite sides of the world. She was in the UAE, far from home, far from her family, working in a foreign country during a global pandemic. I was in England, watching the world collapse from my bedroom window, feeling helpless and uncertain.

The fear of losing my job became real too. When lockdown hit, people everywhere were losing their jobs overnight. Businesses closed. Entire industries shut down. Every day, the news showed more layoffs, more closures, more people suddenly without income. It felt like the world was collapsing economically as much as medically.

I worked on a food packing line — and because it was food, we were considered essential.

We stayed open.
 We kept working.
 We didn't shut down.

But that didn't mean we weren't scared. Every shift felt like walking into the unknown. We didn't know how dangerous it was. We didn't know if we were safe. And even though we were "essential," there was still this fear in the back of my mind:

What if they close us next?
 What if I lose my job?
 What if I couldn't support us anymore?

Maria and I were saving for our future — for flights, for meeting, for everything we dreamed of. Losing my job would have crushed that. It would have pushed everything further away.

But somehow, we were lucky. My workplace stayed open. My wages kept coming in. We could still save for us. That stability — that tiny piece of normality — became something we clung to. It gave us hope when everything else felt uncertain.

But as if the world shutting down wasn't enough, something else hit us — something we didn't expect, something that hurt more than we admitted.

Maria's WiFi connection became a nightmare.

The family she worked for had a teenage son who stayed up all night playing online games. He used it so much that eventually the parents moved the router to a different part of the house — away from Maria's room.

And just like that, our video calls disappeared.

Some weeks we couldn't call at all. Sometimes it was two or three weeks. One time, nearly two months went by without a proper video call.

We went from seeing each other's faces every day to staring at a loading screen, a frozen image, or nothing. Maria could only message me when she was working in other areas of the house — but that was when I was at work. I couldn't reply instantly like before. I couldn't be there in the same way. Our timing was completely out of sync.

It wasn't anyone's fault, but it hurt us deeply.

We missed each other.
We felt the distance more sharply.
We felt disconnected at the worst possible time — when everything else was already falling apart.

But even through the frustration, the silence, the missed calls, and the long gaps, we held on. We didn't give up. We didn't walk away. We waited for each other, even when it was painful.

And that's how we survived the early months of COVID — not perfectly. Not easily. But together.

When she felt scared, she came to me.
 When I felt overwhelmed, I went to her.
 When the world felt too heavy, we held each other up through a screen —
even when the screen barely worked at all.

COVID took away normal life, but it gave us something else — a deeper
connection, a stronger bond, a quiet certainty that we were in this
together, no matter how far apart we were.

By the end of March 2020, the world was shut down. Travel was
impossible. The future was uncertain.

But one thing was clear:

We weren't going anywhere.
 Not from each other.

The world was closing its doors — but somehow, our hearts were opening
wider than ever.

CHAPTER SEVEN

October to December 2020: The Year That Wouldn't Break Us

The months after the world shut down passed in a strange blur. April, May, June, July — they blurred into one. Days melted together. The world went quiet. Life shrank. But through it all, Maria and I stayed steady. We talked every day, even if it wasn't the same as before. We held onto each other through the uncertainty, even when the world felt like it was collapsing.

But something had changed between us — not emotionally, but practically.

The connection problems that started during the early lockdown didn't go away. In fact, they got worse. The family she worked for had moved the WiFi router to stop their teenage son from staying up all night gaming. It solved their problem, but it created a new one for us. The signal barely reached Maria's room anymore. Some days she had no connection at all. Some weeks we couldn't video call. Once, it stretched into nearly two months without seeing each other's faces.

We went from daily video calls to long stretches of silence, broken only by messages she could send when she was working in other parts of the house. But those messages came during the day — when I was at work. I couldn't reply instantly like before. I couldn't be there in the same way. Our timing was completely off.

It wasn't anyone's fault — but it still hurt more than we admitted.

We missed each other. We felt the distance more sharply. We felt disconnected at the worst possible moment — when the world was already falling apart.

And then October arrived — our one-year anniversary.

It wasn't the anniversary we imagined. No dinner. No trip. No physical presence. Just two people in two different countries, celebrating a milestone through a screen that barely worked.

But I wanted to make it special. I needed her to feel loved — even from thousands of miles away.

So I made her something from the heart.

A scrapbook.

Not a quick one. Not a rushed one. A full year of us — printed, arranged, and built page by page. I bought a small camera that printed photos slightly bigger than passport size. I printed our funniest moments — the games, the silly faces, the late-night calls — memories only we understood. I started from the very beginning — the dating site — and built our story in order, month by month.

I added song lyrics too. The songs we sent each other. The ones that meant something. The ones that carried us through the hardest days.

I added photos of us as kids — her childhood, mine — the people we were before we met, and the people we were becoming together.

And on the back page, I added a photo of the promise rings.

It was a gift made with intention, with care, with love. A gift I poured my heart into.

But when the anniversary came… I couldn't give it to her. I held it in my hands, and she saw it only through a video call — a gift made with love — trapped behind a screen.

Even so, she lit up. She loved it. She felt it. I even made a YouTube video showing how I created it — the process, the effort, the joy of building something for her. It was fun. It was meaningful. It was ours.

And the moment she finally held it — the real reaction — wouldn't happen until much later, in a moment that would change everything for us.

Soon after the one-year anniversary of when we first met online, something shifted inside me — not because of anything dramatic, but because of everything we had already survived. The distance, the silence, the dropped calls, the uncertainty… none of it pushed us apart. If anything, it made my feelings clearer. I had been thinking about a future with her since the very beginning. Even in those early months, before the world shut down, before we knew what was coming, something in me already knew she was different.

So I did something I hadn't told anyone about.

I bought an engagement ring.

By then, the shops were shut again. The world was still half-open, half-closed, constantly changing its rules. So instead of walking into a jeweller and choosing something in person, I sat alone in my room late at night, scrolling through websites, comparing designs, reading reviews, trying to find something that felt right. It wasn't the romantic moment people imagine when they think of engagement rings. There was no jeweller, no counter, no bright lights. Just me, a desktop computer, and a decision that felt bigger than the world outside.

But in a strange way, it made the moment more real. More intentional. We had already talked about marriage. We had talked about our future — the kind of life we wanted, the kind of family we hoped to build. We even talked about children. She always said she wanted a boy, someone like me. And I always said I wanted a girl, someone like her. These were the kinds of conversations you only have when the future feels real — solid, possible, worth waiting for. She had even given me her ring measurements months earlier, back when the idea of getting engaged felt like a dream we didn't know when the world would allow.

So when I found the right ring, I didn't hesitate. I ordered it, waited for the delivery, and hid it away the moment it arrived. I didn't know when I'd be able to give it to her — when flights would return, when borders would open, when the world would finally let us be in the same room again. But I knew one thing with absolute clarity: she was the one.

A promise waiting for the right moment. A future waiting for the world to catch up.

December came, and 2020 still wasn't finished with us.

My whole family got COVID. It hit fast. One day my parents were fine, and the next they were coughing, exhausted, struggling to get out of bed. The house felt heavy, quiet, and frightening. I was scared — not for myself, but for them.

Maria was there for me through every moment. She checked on me constantly. She worried with me. She prayed for my parents. She became my emotional support when I felt helpless watching the people I loved suffer.

And then Christmas approached.

Normally, my parents put up the tree early. It was tradition — the lights, the decorations, the warmth. But this year, they were too sick. The living room stayed dark. The boxes of decorations stayed untouched. The house felt empty.

But my mum... she wasn't having it.

Even though she was still recovering, she was determined that Christmas wasn't going to disappear. She gathered the strength she had, and with the help of my brother and my brother-in-law, she put the tree up just before Christmas.

I filmed the whole thing for our YouTube channel — and Maria watched it all live on video call. She saw my mum slowly unpack the decorations. She saw my brother and brother-in-law helping her steady the tree. She saw the effort, the love, the determination to make Christmas happen despite everything.

It wasn't polished or perfect — it was real.

A tired mum refusing to let illness steal the holiday. A family pulling together in the middle of a hard moment. A small act of hope in a house that had felt heavy for weeks.

We called the video "Saving Christmas."

When the tree was finally lit, the house felt alive again. Warm again. Like home again. And Maria, watching through a screen from thousands of miles away, felt like she was right there with us — part of my family, part of my world.

By the end of December, my parents recovered. The house healed. My heart healed. And Maria and I ended the year stronger than ever.

2020 tried to break us.
 Instead, it proved something:
 We could survive anything — as long as we were together.

CHAPTER EIGHT

Early 2021: The Slow Return of Hope

The year began with sickness, but it slowly turned into the year of possibility.

2021 didn't start with fireworks or celebration. It started with me getting COVID.

After everything my family had gone through in December, after watching my parents struggle and after the fear that filled the house, I thought maybe we were finally safe. But in January 2021, it was my turn. I tested positive, and suddenly the world shrank again — into isolation, worry, and the heavy atmosphere we'd just escaped.

Maria was terrified for me.

She messaged constantly, checking if I was breathing okay, if I had a fever, if I was eating. Even with the connection problems, even with the router still in the wrong place, she found ways to reach me. Her messages sometimes arrived hours late, sometimes all at once, but they always came. And that was enough.

Being sick made the distance feel sharper.

I wanted her there.
 I wanted her voice, her face, her comfort.

But the connection still wasn't strong enough for video calls.

So we did what we always did — we adapted.

I recovered slowly, and by the time February arrived, the world was talking about vaccines. It felt like the first real sign of hope in a long time. People were still scared, still unsure, but there was a sense that maybe — just maybe — life could start moving again.

I booked my first vaccine appointment, but because I'd had COVID, I had to cancel it and rebook for a later date. It felt like everything in this pandemic came with delays, setbacks, and waiting. But eventually, the day came.

And I filmed it.

I made a YouTube video about getting the vaccine — not because I wanted views, but because it felt like a moment worth documenting. A moment that said, "We're getting closer. We're getting through this."

Maria was on call with me while I went. Even with the weak, glitchy connection, she stayed with me. She wanted to be part of it. She wanted to see me take that step toward safety, toward our future, toward the day we could finally meet.

I remember sitting in the waiting area, phone in my hand, her voice crackling through the speaker.

She was nervous for me.
 I was nervous too.

But it felt like something important — like a door opening after a year of closed ones.

When the needle went in, she let out a tiny breath of relief.

And I smiled, because even though she wasn't physically there, she was with me in the only way she could be.

After that, early 2021 settled into a slow, steady rhythm. The world was still cautious, still recovering, but things were changing: vaccines were rolling out, restrictions were easing, travel rules were updating, and people were talking about the future again.

And for the first time in a long time, the idea of meeting didn't feel like a fantasy.

It felt possible.

We started talking about dates again. We started imagining what it would be like. We started counting months instead of years.

The connection problems were still there — some weeks we barely managed a call, some days we only exchanged a few messages — but the emotional distance was gone. We were aligned again. We were moving toward something real.

Early 2021 wasn't dramatic.
 It wasn't chaotic like 2020.
 It was quiet, steady, hopeful.

It was the chapter where the world began to heal.

And so did we.

For the first time in months, meeting her felt possible again. December 2021 — the month we might finally meet — was coming into view.

CHAPTER NINE

Delays, Distance, and the Week the World Finally Let Us Breathe

By mid-2021, we were holding onto one thing:
December 2021.
Our month.
Our plan — December 2021.
The moment we would finally meet in person.

It gave us direction.
It gave us hope.
It gave us something solid in a world that kept shifting under our feet.

But life — as always — had other ideas.

Maria was supposed to go home to the Philippines in September 2021.
That was the date everything was meant to change.

Her contract in the UAE would end, she'd finally be free from the long hours and strict household, and she'd be back with her family.

We imagined it so many times:

Her stepping off the plane.
Her hugging her parents.

Her starting her new chapter back home.
Her finally having the time and space for us again.

But the world was still tangled in COVID rules and chaos.

Flights kept getting cancelled.
Schedules kept shifting.
Airlines kept pushing her date further and further away.

She was vaccinated — she just couldn't find the proof.
Her employer had misplaced her documentation.

Without it, she would have had to quarantine when she arrived in the Philippines.

But even that wasn't the real problem.

The real problem was simple:

Her flight kept getting cancelled.

Every week she would message me:

"Matt... maybe next week."
"Matt... they cancelled again."
"Matt... I'm scared I'll never get home."

And every time, I felt the same sinking feeling —
the same frustration,
the same helplessness,
the same ache of wanting to fix something I had no control over.

It wasn't just frustrating.
It was heartbreaking.

She wanted to go home.
I wanted her to go home.
We needed her to go home so our plan could finally begin.

September passed.
October passed.
November passed.

And finally — after months of delays and stress —
she got a confirmed flight.

She flew home in December 2021, three months later than planned.

But she made it.

And that was all that mattered.

Long before she finally flew home, we had already started something new
together — something that became a lifeline for both of us.

A YouTube channel.

We created it back in November 2019, long before the world shut down.

It wasn't random.
It wasn't a hobby.

It was a plan — a way to build something together, even from two
different countries.

We watched other long-distance couples on YouTube:

Couples who had never met.
Couples who waited years.
Couples who fought through borders and visas and distance.
Couples who proved that love could survive anything.

One night we said:

"If they can do it... why can't we?"

So we filmed our lives —
her in the UAE,
me in the UK —
and we built something together.

Slowly, painfully slowly, the channel grew.

It took five months before anything happened.

Five months of effort.
Five months of waiting.
Five months of hoping.

Then, finally...

We got monetized.

December 2021 — the same month she finally got her flight home.

It felt like the universe giving us a sign.

A small one, but a sign all the same.

And then something incredible happened.

In the first three months — January, February, March 2022 —
 the channel earned £1,200.

Every penny of it, I sent to Maria.

Not because she asked.
 Not because she expected it.

But because she wanted the channel to help her stay home,
 to rest,
 to be with her family,
 to have time for us.

And because I wanted that too.

If she had to go back to 12-hour shifts,
 we would barely speak.

We would lose the connection we had fought so hard to protect.

Supporting her wasn't a burden.

It was a choice.
 It was a commitment.
 It was a promise.

A promise that distance wouldn't break us.
 A promise that we would keep building our future.
 A promise that we were in this together.

To make matters worse, there had been a huge Typhoon in the Philippines
and Maria had lost connection with her family due to that storm a few
days before her flight. I had been following the aftermath of it online.

When she finally landed in Manila, something happened that neither of us
expected.

Her phone connected.
 Messages came through.

Her family had a signal again at home.

They were safe.

The house had taken a hit —
 a fallen tree was leaning against one wall, cracking it, pushing it inward —
 but it was repairable.

She sent me photos from her hotel room.

The damage looked frightening at first, but they were already planning
repairs.

After weeks of silence and fear, that one message felt like the world finally
let us breathe again.

She had to quarantine in Manila for a full week.

She spent seven days in a hotel room, alone, exhausted, and emotionally drained.

But something beautiful happened there.

Every morning, when she opened the blinds, a small bird sat on the window ledge — singing, waiting, unafraid.

It never flew away, even when she stood close.

It was the first gentle thing she had experienced in months.

And for the first time in so long, we had clear WiFi.

No lag.
 No dropped calls.
 No interruptions.

It was Christmas week, and I was off work.

She was in quarantine.

We had nowhere to go, nothing pulling us away.

So we spent the entire week together — literally 24 hours a day — on video call.

If she ate, I stayed on.
 If I watched a movie, she stayed on.
 If one of us moved to another room, the call stayed open.

We lived our separate lives, but we lived them together.

It was simple.
It was quiet.
It was sweet.
It was ours.

After quarantine, she travelled home to her family.

A few days later, she went to Dumaguete and checked into a hotel — just so we could have privacy, time, and space to reconnect properly.

For the first time in months, it felt like the world wasn't fighting us.

It felt like we had survived something heavy.

It felt like we were finally stepping into the next chapter.

We didn't know it yet, but the hardest part of 2021 was behind us.

And the hardest part of our entire journey was still to come.

CHAPTER TEN

The Calm Before the Message

When Maria finally returned home after months of delays, cancellations, and fear, something inside both of us settled.
For the first time in what felt like forever, life didn't feel like a crisis we were trying to survive.

It felt... normal.
Soft.
Steady.

We had a rhythm again.

I worked my shifts.
She spent time with her family.

And every day, without fail, we were together on a video call — not fighting for signal, not losing connection, not counting minutes before she had to run back to work.

Just us.
Finally.

Being back in the Philippines meant she could show me her world again — the real one, not the rushed glimpses from her old life in the UAE.

She walked me through her home, room by room.
 She showed me the street outside, the neighbours, the little details that made up her everyday life.

And then she took me to the beach.

Her beach.

The one just outside her house.

The water was calm, the sky wide and open, and from that shoreline you could see Turtle Island — a small shape rising from the sea — and beyond it, the larger Danjugan Island.

She told me she had never been there.
 She said she'd like to go one day.

I didn't know it then, but that small moment — that quiet wish — would become something much bigger later.
 Something life-changing.

But for now, it was just a dream she shared with me, standing barefoot on the sand with the wind in her hair, the sea behind her, and the islands in the distance.

Those weeks after she got home were some of the sweetest moments of our entire long-distance journey.

There was relief.
There was peace.
There was time.

Time to talk.
Time to laugh.
Time to breathe.
Time to feel like a real couple again.

We weren't rushing.
We weren't panicking.
We weren't fighting the world.

We were just living — together, even from two different countries.

And with that calm came clarity.

December 2022 was our plan.
Our goal.
Our meeting point.
The moment everything would finally come together.

We held onto that date like it was a promise written in stone.

Then — just when everything felt steady — something unexpected happened.

A message.

A simple notification that popped up on my phone one ordinary day, cutting through the quiet routine we had built.

At first, I didn't think much of it.
 It looked like spam.
 Or a mistake.
 Or something meant for someone else.

But it wasn't.

It was from a casting team.

For a show on TV.

They wanted to talk to us.
 They wanted to hear our story.
 They wanted to know if we were interested.

I stared at the message for a long time, not quite believing it.

We hadn't applied for anything.
 We hadn't reached out.
 We hadn't even thought about being on a show.

It just... appeared.

Out of nowhere.

Like the universe had tapped us on the shoulder.

I didn't know what to make of it.
 I didn't know why it had come to us, or what it meant, or what we were
supposed to do with it.

All I knew was that life had finally settled, finally softened, finally given us room to breathe — and now something new was knocking at the door.

Something unexpected.
Something we hadn't asked for.
Something that felt strangely timed.

I didn't fully open it.
Not yet.
I just stared at the screen, feeling the quiet shift in the air — the sense that our story, which had been moving so slowly and gently, might be about to change direction.

I didn't know how.
I didn't know why.
I didn't know what would come next.

But I felt it.

A spark.
A pull.
A question forming in the back of my mind.

Not fear.
Not excitement.

Just... possibility.

A sense that whatever this was, it wasn't random.

And that was where the calm ended — not with chaos, not with panic, but with a single, unexpected message that would lead us somewhere we never imagined.

Somewhere we didn't even know existed yet.

Life was about to change again, in ways we never saw coming.

CHAPTER ELEVEN

The Comment That Changed Everything

The message that appeared at the end of Chapter Ten didn't come out of nowhere — not really.
 It came from a moment so small I barely remembered it at first.

A moment that felt harmless, ordinary, almost forgettable.

A Facebook comment.

That was all it took.

It happened weeks earlier, on a day when I was scrolling through a long-distance relationship group — one of those places where people shared their victories, heartbreaks, countdowns, and airport reunions.

I liked reading those posts.
 They made the distance feel less impossible.

Someone had posted that they were finally about to meet their long-distance partner for the first time.

Their excitement was contagious.
 Their hope felt familiar.

So I commented.

Just a simple message about us — about how Maria and I were planning to meet in December 2022 because the Philippines was still closed and flights were impossible.

Nothing dramatic.
Nothing attention seeking.
Just honesty.

I didn't think about it again.
I didn't expect anything from it.
I didn't even check back to see if anyone replied.

It was just a comment.

But someone saw it.

Someone who wasn't just another LDR couple.
Someone who wasn't just scrolling for comfort or community.

Someone from a casting team.

Weeks later — after Maria had returned home, after our connection had stabilised, after life had finally softened — that's when the message arrived.

And now, reading it properly, everything clicked into place.

They had found us because of that comment.
They had read our story.
They had followed the thread.
They had reached out because something about us stood out.

They asked if I was still with Maria.
 They said they were working on a TV programme about long-distance couples.

They explained the concept — me flying to the Philippines for four days and Maria flying to the UK for four days, our first meeting documented, our story shared with the world.

It didn't feel real.

I stood there staring at my phone, with my heart pounding, trying to make sense of it.

We hadn't applied.
 We hadn't contacted anyone.
 We hadn't even known a show like this existed.

But they wanted us.

Us.

I told Maria immediately.

I didn't hide it.
 I didn't soften it.
 I didn't try to figure it out alone.

"Babe… a programme contacted me."

Her reply came instantly.

"What programme? Why?"

I explained everything — the message, the idea, the opportunity, the possibility of meeting earlier than planned.

She didn't panic.
 She didn't shut down.
 She didn't tell me to ignore it.

She listened.

Then she said the words that hit me harder than the message itself:

"It's up to you... you decide."

Her trust was overwhelming.

She didn't know what would happen.
 She didn't know how the world would react.
 She didn't know what being on a show would mean for us.

But she trusted me.
 She trusted us.

And that trust felt bigger than the opportunity itself.

That night, I lay in bed staring at the ceiling, replaying everything in my mind.

The ring.
 The plan.
 The £1,200 I sent her.
 The cancelled flights.
 The delays.

The December 2022 reunion.
The future we were building.

And now this —

a chance to meet earlier,
a chance to change everything,
a chance to tell our story to the world.

It felt terrifying.
It felt overwhelming.
It felt like a turning point.

I imagined stepping off a plane in the Philippines.
I imagined seeing her for the first time.
I imagined cameras, interviews, strangers watching our story unfold.
I imagined the moment our online world became real.

But deep down, beneath the nerves and the uncertainty, I knew
something:

This wasn't about TV.
This wasn't about attention.
This wasn't about being seen.

This was about us.

Our journey.
Our love.
Our future.

And maybe — just maybe —

this was the next step in the story we were meant to tell.

Two hearts.
 Two countries.
 One comment —

and everything began to shift.

CHAPTER TWELVE

The First Interview

The message from the programme had already shifted something in my life, but the moment they scheduled the first Skype call... that's when everything became real.

It wasn't just a possibility anymore.
It wasn't just a "maybe."
It wasn't just an interesting message in my inbox.

This was movement.
This was momentum.
This was the first step toward something that could change everything.

And even though nothing was guaranteed, the call felt big.
Bigger than I expected.

It was just me on that first one.
Maria's interview would come later.

I remember sitting there, waiting for the screen to connect, trying to look calm even though my heart was pounding.

My palms were sweating.
I kept checking my hair in the camera preview like a teenager before a first date.

And then suddenly — there they were.

Smiling.
 Friendly.
 Genuinely interested.

They asked how Maria and I met.
 They asked about our long-distance relationship.
 They asked about the challenges, the waiting, the distance.

And then came the questions that weren't about romance —
 the questions meant to test the story.

"What do you think will happen when you get there?"
 "Do you think she'll turn up?"
 "Have you ever wondered if she wasn't real?"

I understood why they were asking.

They weren't being rude — they were doing their job.
 They weren't just looking for love stories.
 They were looking for tension, uncertainty, the kind of things that make
"good TV."

But with us, they weren't getting that.

So I told them the truth.

"We've been together since 2019," I said.
 "I've never doubted her — not once."

They watched me closely, waiting for a hesitation.

There wasn't any.

And then, because it was the most honest thing I could say, I added:

"I already have the engagement ring."

Their reaction was instant — surprised, excited, genuinely pleased.

Then came the follow-up:

"Does she know you have it?"
 "And does she know you'd take it with you... if you were selected?"

And that was where the truth mattered.

"She knows I have the ring," I said.
 "But she doesn't know I'd take it."

Because in her heart, Maria wanted so much to come to the UK first.

She wanted to meet my mum and dad.
 She had been texting my mum regularly, building a relationship with her long before she ever met me in person.

She imagined the proposal happening here — in the UK — surrounded by the family she hoped to join.

She even told me not to take the ring yet.
 She wanted me to wait until she was here.

But I knew the reality.

Getting a UK visa wasn't easy.
 Even a visit visa was complicated.

And if she was denied, that denial would stay on her record for future applications.

So I couldn't risk waiting.

From the moment I bought the ring, I knew I was going to propose on my first trip to the Philippines.

Not because I didn't respect her wishes — but because I wanted to protect our future.

And because proposing there, in her home, would be a genuine surprise.

Her answer was already yes.

But the moment had to be right.

They listened closely — not for drama, not for a storyline, but because they could see the truth in what I was saying.

Then they asked:

"Do you have the ring with you?
 Could we see it?"

I didn't hesitate.

I reached over, picked up the ring box, and held it up to the camera.

Right there, live on the call.

Their faces lit up — not in a staged way, but in a real, human way.

They could see the ring.
 They could see the seriousness.
 They could see the future I was planning.

Then came the question that made everything feel suddenly real:

"Would you take the ring with you... if you're selected?"

And I said exactly what was in my heart:

"Yes.
 The moment I bought the ring, I knew I was going to ask her on the
December trip.
 So if your trip happens first...
 why wouldn't I ask her then?"

And then I added, without even thinking:

"Our plan was to get married in December this year...
 or at least to seriously look at the possibility."

They weren't expecting that.

I could see it in their faces — the surprise, the warmth, the sense that this
wasn't just a story.

This was real.
 This was love.
 This was a future already forming.

And I think that moment mattered.

Not because of the show —
 but because they realised something:

We weren't going to give them drama.
 We weren't going to give them arguments.
 We weren't going to give them a "maybe she won't turn up" storyline.

We were a real couple.

And they saw that early on.

When the call ended, I sat there for a moment, letting it all sink in.

Nothing was confirmed.
 Nothing was promised.

But something inside me had shifted.

The interview didn't give me certainty.
 It gave me clarity.

We were ready.
 We were real.

And whatever happened next...
 I knew we had shown them exactly who we were.

CHAPTER THIRTEEN

The Months Between

The months that followed were strange in a way I had never experienced before.

Not quiet.
 Not empty.
 Not silent.

But uncertain.

It felt like living in a waiting room between two versions of my life — the one I had and the one I knew was coming.

Nothing dramatic happened.
 Nothing explosive.
 Nothing chaotic.

But everything felt different.

They stayed in touch.
 They asked questions.
 They wanted long conversations.

They wanted to understand us — really understand us.

They wanted to see how we spoke about each other, how we planned, how we dreamed, how we imagined our future.

It wasn't dramatic.
It wasn't chaotic.
It wasn't emotional fireworks.

It was steady.
It was honest.
It was real.

And I think that's what surprised them.

They asked things like:

"How do you see your future together?"
"What do you think will happen when you meet?"
"Do you ever worry she won't turn up?"
"Do you ever doubt she's real?"

But these weren't questions about us.

These were questions about storylines — the kind of uncertainty they expected from long-distance couples.

The kind of drama they were used to.

But with us, they didn't get that.

Because we weren't guessing.
We weren't hoping blindly.
We weren't imagining a fantasy.

We had been together since 2019.

We had built a life in messages, calls, routines, rituals, and plans.

We had involved our families.
 We had talked about marriage.
 We had talked about the future from the moment she replied to my first message.

We were a real couple.

And they saw that early on.

But even with all the conversations, all the follow-ups, all the questions...

there was still silence.

Weeks passed.
 Then months.

From March to July, we heard nothing official.

No confirmation.
 No rejection.
 Just waiting.

But deep down, something settled quietly inside me.

A certainty.
 A feeling I couldn't shake.

They were going to choose us.

Not because I was confident on camera — I wasn't.
Not because I was trying to impress them — I wasn't.
Not because we were dramatic — we weren't.

But because they needed us.

They needed a real couple.
They needed a real love story.
They needed something grounded, something pure, something true.

And that was us.

Maria and I talked about it so many times:

"Surely they see we're real."
"Surely they feel our connection."
"Surely they understand our story is different."

We didn't know anything about the other couples at that point.
We didn't know their stories or their situations.

But even now, looking back, it's obvious:

What would the show have been without Matt and Maria?

By the time July arrived, the waiting had become its own chapter in our story.

A chapter of patience.
A chapter of quiet confidence.
A chapter of preparation for a future we could feel, even if we couldn't see it yet.

And then — just when the silence felt like it might last forever —

the message came.

A Skype call.

Both of us invited.

And that moment...

that moment would become the opening of Chapter Fourteen.

The moment everything changed.

CHAPTER FOURTEEN

The Decision

The moment the Skype screen loaded, I knew this wasn't another check-in.

It wasn't another round of questions.
It wasn't another "getting to know you" call.
It wasn't another test of our story.

Because this time, Maria's face appeared beside mine.

It was me, her, and the producers — all on the same call.

The second I saw her there, sitting in her room in the Philippines, smiling nervously at the camera, something inside me shifted.

This was it.
This was the moment.

They didn't waste time.
They didn't build suspense.
They didn't drag it out.

They looked at us — really looked — and then said the words we had been waiting months to hear:

"You've been selected."

And then:

"You're the main couple."

For a second, everything went quiet.

Not on the call, but in me.

I didn't gasp.
 I didn't freeze.
 I didn't even look surprised.

I just smiled.

Because I had known it before they said it.

I had felt it in the months of silence.
 I had sensed it in the way they kept coming back to us.
 I had seen it in the way they reacted to our interviews.

Maria covered her mouth with her hand, eyes wide, trying not to cry.

I could see her shaking slightly — overwhelmed, relieved, stunned.

But as for me?

I felt calm.
 Steady.
 Grounded.

Because this wasn't a shock.

This was confirmation.

Confirmation of everything I had believed.
 Confirmation of everything we had built.
 Confirmation of everything we had held onto through years of distance, lockdowns, delays, and uncertainty.

They kept talking — explaining the next steps, the logistics, the filming schedule, the travel possibilities — but I barely heard any of it.

All I could think was:

It's happening.
 It's finally happening.
 We're going to meet.

Not in December.
 Not after years of waiting.
 Not after all the delays and cancellations.

Soon.
 Earlier than planned.
 Earlier than expected.
 Earlier than we ever dared to imagine.

I looked at Maria on the screen — her eyes shining, her smile trembling — and I felt something I hadn't felt in years.

A sense of inevitability.

Like the universe had finally stopped delaying us.
 Like the world had finally opened its doors.
 Like everything we had survived had led to this exact moment.

When the call ended, I didn't move for a few seconds.

I just sat there, letting it sink in.

We were chosen.
 We were the main couple.
 We were going to meet.

And for the first time since 2019, the future wasn't a distant dream.

It was real.
 It was close. It was coming.

This was the moment everything shifted — not because they picked us, but because the waiting was finally over.

The countdown had begun.

CHAPTER FIFTEEN

The Countdown Begins

When the call ended, the world didn't explode into fireworks.

It didn't erupt into noise or celebration.
It didn't feel chaotic or overwhelming.

It felt still.

Still in the way a moment feels when it's too big for your body to process all at once.
Still in the way the air feels right before a storm breaks.
Still in the way truth settles — quietly, deeply, without asking permission.

We were chosen.
We were the main couple.

And for the first time since 2019, the future wasn't a distant idea.

It was real.
It was happening.
It was coming fast.

Maria messaged me the second the call ended.

Her words were a rush — excitement, nerves, disbelief, joy — all tangled together.

But underneath it, I could feel something deeper, something steady:

She felt seen.
She felt valued.
She felt like our story mattered.

And I felt the same.

For days, the adrenaline didn't fade.

Everything felt sharper — colours, sounds, even the way people spoke to me at work.

It was like the world had shifted a few degrees, and I was finally standing in the place I'd been walking toward for years.

But once the excitement settled, the practical reality hit me with full force.

I wasn't imagining anymore.
I wasn't planning someday.
I wasn't dreaming in the abstract.

I was preparing.

Preparing to travel 7,000 miles.
Preparing to meet the woman I loved.
Preparing to step into a moment that would change everything.
Preparing to propose.

The ring became the centre of everything.

Not because I doubted it was there — I checked it constantly anyway —
but because it represented the future I was about to step into.

Maria still believed the proposal would happen in the UK.

She imagined meeting my mum and dad first.
 She imagined standing in my world, seeing my life, and being welcomed
into my family.

She had even told me not to take the ring yet.
 She wanted me to wait until she was here.

But I carried the truth quietly.

A UK visa wasn't guaranteed.
 Even a visit visa was complicated.

And a denial would follow her for years.

I couldn't risk waiting.
 I couldn't risk losing the moment.
 I couldn't risk letting paperwork decide our future.

So long before the show ever contacted us, I had already made my choice:

I would propose on my first trip to the Philippines.

No matter what.

Not out of defiance.
 Not out of impatience.

But out of love — the kind that protects the future before it arrives.

Her answer was already yes.

But the moment had to be perfect.

In the days that followed, our conversations shifted.

They became softer, deeper, more intimate — not romantic, but emotional in a way that only anticipation can create.

We talked about the first moment we'd see each other.

Back when December was the plan, we imagined the arrivals hall — the noise, the crowd, the chaos, the moment our eyes found each other after years of waiting.

Maria told me she might feel shy about kissing fully at first.

Not because she didn't want to — she did — but because it would feel overwhelming.

Too big.
 Too real.
 Too much emotion hitting all at once after years of distance.

And I understood that completely.

Because I knew the moment I saw her, everything inside me would shift too.

The waiting would end.
 The distance would break.
 The future would begin.

And now, for the first time, the countdown had truly started.

CHAPTER SIXTEEN

The Final Preparations

The days after the decision call felt different — not louder, not chaotic, but sharper.

Colours looked brighter.
 Sounds felt clearer.
 Even the air seemed to carry a new kind of energy.

It was as if the world had shifted a few degrees, and I was finally standing in the place I had been walking toward for years.

Because now, I wasn't dreaming.
 I wasn't planning.
 I wasn't imagining.

I was preparing.

Preparing to travel 7,000 miles.
 Preparing to meet the woman I loved.
 Preparing to step into a moment that would change everything.

The first problem was simple:

I had nothing to wear.

The Philippines wasn't just warm — it was hot, humid, tropical.

A world away from rainy-day Britain, where even in summer you keep a jacket nearby "just in case."

I didn't own a single pair of shorts.
 Not one.

No light shirts.
 No sandals.
 No clothes that made sense for the 35°C heat and blinding sunshine.

My wardrobe was built for clouds, drizzle, and grey skies — not for a country where the sun feels like it's sitting on your shoulder.

So Maria helped me with everything.

We went through photos, links, colours, and styles.

She told me what would be comfortable, what would suit the weather, what would look good on me.

She helped me choose shorts, T-shirts, sandals, light clothes — things I had never worn before but would need the moment I stepped off the plane.

She even helped me pick a new bag, something practical for travel, something that would survive airports, heat, and long days of filming.

It felt like another layer of connection between us.

She wasn't just helping me shop — she was helping me prepare to enter her world.

And somehow, buying those simple things made everything feel even more real.

Then there were the gifts.

Over the years, I had collected things for her — birthday cards, Christmas cards, small presents, little pieces of my life I had always planned to give her "one day."

But "one day" had never come.

Now it was coming all at once.

I gathered everything I had saved — the cards I had written but never sent, the gifts I had bought but never delivered, the things I had kept safe through lockdowns, delays, and years of waiting.

Packing them felt emotional in a way I didn't expect.

It felt like I was packing the years themselves — all the moments we missed, all the celebrations we couldn't share, all the love that had been waiting for its moment.

And now that moment was finally here.

The next problem was the passport.

I hadn't had one in fifteen years.

It had been lost long ago, and I never replaced it because I never imagined I'd need it.

But the moment the show first contacted me — long before we were chosen — I ordered a new one.

And now, as the days ticked down, I kept checking the post like my life depended on it.

Every morning I'd check for the post, heart pounding, hoping to see that envelope.

Every day it didn't arrive, the tension grew.

It was the one thing I couldn't control.
 The one thing that could stop everything.

But I held onto the belief that it would come in time — because everything else in our story had arrived exactly when it needed to.

As the trip became real, our conversations shifted again.

We talked about the journey — the flights, the airports, the heat, the nerves.

We imagined the moment I'd land, the moment I'd walk toward her, the moment everything would finally become real.

She imagined me walking toward her.
 She imagined the first hug.
 She imagined the life we'd start building from that moment forward.

And every message between us felt heavier, more meaningful, more electric.

We didn't know the filming schedule yet.
 We didn't know they would start at sunrise and end at sunset.
 We didn't know how intense it would be, how little time we'd have alone,
how much of our story would be lived in front of cameras.

We thought we'd have long days together, exploring, talking, catching up
on years of distance.

We didn't realise that most of our daylight hours would belong to the
show.

But we also didn't know something else — something more important:

Even if we only had the darkness together,
 being together created enough light for us.

We didn't say it like that at the time.
 But we felt it.

The days that followed were a blur of preparation.

I laid everything out on the bed — clothes, documents, gifts, chargers,
toiletries, the new bag, the sandals, the shirts Maria helped me choose.

I checked everything twice.
 Then again.
 Then again.

I rehearsed the journey in my head — the airport, the flight, the arrival, the
moment I'd see her.

I imagined the first hug.
 The first touch.
 The first moment of silence where we'd just look at each other and know:

We made it.

I checked the ring again.

Not because I doubted it was there — but because it represented everything that was coming.

The future.
 The promise.
 The moment I had been carrying in my heart for years.

As the final days approached, the countdown became real.

Every morning felt like one step closer.
 Every night felt like one day less.

And the truth settled in quietly, steadily, completely:

The next chapter began at sunrise.

CHAPTER SEVENTEEN

The Morning of the Trip

I woke before my alarm.

Not because I was nervous.
 Not because I was scared.

But because something inside me already knew:

Today was the day.

The room was still dark, the kind of quiet that only exists in the early hours before the world wakes up.

For a moment, I just lay there, listening to my own breathing, letting the reality settle in.

This was the last morning I would wake up in a world where Maria existed only on a screen.

By tonight, I would be in the air.
 By tomorrow, I will be in her country.

And soon after that, I would be standing in front of her — real, physical, close enough to touch.

The thought hit me with a force that made my chest tighten.

This is happening.

I sat up slowly, letting the moment wash over me.

The suitcase was already packed, sitting open by the door like a quiet promise.

The new clothes Maria helped me choose were folded neatly inside.
 The gifts I had saved for years were wrapped and ready.

The new passport — the one I had waited for with my heart in my throat — was tucked safely into the front pocket of my bag.

And the ring...

The ring was exactly where it needed to be.

I picked it up, held it in my hand for a moment, feeling the weight of everything it represented.

The future.
 The promise.
 The moment that was coming.

I didn't open the box.
 I didn't need to.

Just holding it was enough.

When I finally stepped out of my room, I realised I wasn't the only one awake.

The cat and the dog had decided to stage a full protest.

For years now, the three of us had become our own little family.

It still amazes me sometimes how it all started back in 2019, when the cat was just a stray who used to follow Milo and me on our nightly walks to the park.

Milo would stop and look back for him, almost asking me to wait.

Some nights he even asked to go out just so he could see the cat again, like he'd chosen him before I did.

Eventually, I brought him inside.

And from that moment on, the three of us weren't just a man, a dog, and a stray.

We were a family — a proper one — and we had been for years.

They slept in my room every night — one at the foot of the bed, one curled up near my side — as if they'd silently agreed that this was their place, their routine, their home with me.

And now, seeing the bags by the door, they knew something was happening.

My carry-on bag was on the floor, unzipped—and the cat had climbed inside it, curled up like he was ready to be smuggled to the Philippines.

In the other big bag, Milo was sitting squarely in the middle of my clothes, staring up at me with the saddest eyes I had ever seen.

They weren't having it.

The cat blinked at me like "You're not going without me."

Milo looked like he was about to file a formal complaint.

For a moment, I just stood there, taking it in — the ridiculousness, the sweetness, the loyalty.

It grounded me in a way nothing else could.

I knelt down, stroked Milo's head, scratched behind the cat's ears, and whispered that I'd be back.

That this wasn't goodbye.
 That I was going to bring someone home who would love them too.

They didn't move.
 Not an inch.

It was their way of saying they didn't want me to leave them — and somehow, that made the morning feel even more real, even more emotional.

Eventually, I lifted them gently out of the bags, one by one.

They followed me around the house as I got ready, their little paws tapping behind me like a soundtrack to the morning.

I moved through the rest of the morning slowly, deliberately, like each action was part of a ritual.

Shower.
 Shave.

Dress.
Check the bag.
Check the documents.
Check the ring.
Check everything again.

I wasn't rushing.
I wasn't panicking.

I was grounding myself — making sure I was stepping into this day with clarity, not chaos.

Outside, the sky was beginning to lighten, the first hint of sunrise stretching across the horizon.

It felt symbolic, like the world was opening with me.

A new day.
A new chapter.
A new life beginning.

As I zipped the suitcase, a wave of emotion hit me — not fear, not doubt, but something deeper.

This was the moment I had waited for since 2019.

Every message, every call, every birthday we spent apart, every Christmas we promised "next year," every delay, every hope, every moment we held onto each other through distance...

It all led here.

To this morning.
 To this suitcase.
 To this journey.
 To her.

The house was quiet as I stepped into the hallway.

My footsteps felt louder than usual, like the sound carried more meaning.

I paused at the door, with my hand on the handle, letting myself feel the weight of the moment.

When I walked through this door, I wouldn't just be leaving home.

I'd be leaving the version of my life where Maria was far away.

I'd be stepping into the version where she was real, close, tangible — where everything we had imagined would finally become something we could touch.

I took a breath.
 A long, steady one.

Then I opened the door.

The morning air hit me — cool, fresh, alive.

The sky was turning gold.

It felt like the world was saying, "Go."

So I did.

I stepped outside, closed the door behind me, and walked toward the journey that would change everything.

Today, I wasn't waiting anymore.

Today, I was going to her.

CHAPTER EIGHTEEN

The Airport

The drive to the airport felt like moving through a film — familiar streets passing by, but none of them feeling the same anymore.

They felt like the last pages of a chapter I was closing.

By the time the car pulled up outside the terminal, the world around me had shifted into something louder, brighter, faster.

The airport was its own universe — a place where time didn't behave normally, where everyone was rushing somewhere, where the air buzzed with movement and possibility.

But inside, I felt strangely calm.

Not numb.
 Not detached.

Just focused.

Like my mind had narrowed down to a single point:

I'm going to her.

Check-in was quick.
 Bag drop was quicker.

And then came security — the one place where the nerves finally caught up with me.

I placed my jacket and bag on the belt, stepped forward, and suddenly my heart jumped into my throat.

What if the ring was still in my pocket?

I knew it wasn't.
 I had checked it a dozen times that morning.

It was safely in my bag, exactly where it should be.

But in that split second, with people behind me and the security officer watching, I found myself patting my pockets like a man who'd forgotten his own name.

The security guy noticed immediately.

He raised an eyebrow, gave me that half-amused, half-suspicious look, and then wanded me while I was still fiddling with my pockets like an idiot.

It was such a small moment — but it made me laugh inside.

Here I was, about to fly 7,000 miles to propose to the woman I loved, and the thing that nearly sent me into a panic wasn't the flight, or the cameras, or the future...

It was the idea of accidentally sending the engagement ring through airport security.

Once I cleared security, the airport opened up in front of me — bright lights, rolling suitcases, announcements echoing overhead.

People rushing, people waiting, people sleeping, people eating.

But I moved through it with a kind of quiet focus.

Every step felt like a step toward her.
 Every moment felt like a countdown.

When I reached the gate, I finally sat down.

And that was when everything hit me at once.

This was it.

The last moment before everything changed.
 The last moment before I stepped into the life I had been building with Maria for years.

I wasn't nervous.
 I wasn't scared.

I was ready.

Ready in a way I had never been ready for anything in my life.

When the boarding announcement came, I stood up, grabbed my bag, and walked toward the queue.

And then — because of course it would happen to me — as I stepped onto the plane, I bumped my head on the overhead panel.

A solid, unmistakable thud.

I'm six-foot-three.

It's a me thing to do.

I smiled to myself, shaking my head.

If there was ever a moment that summed up who I was — tall, clumsy, hopeful, determined — it was that one.

The flight attendant gave me a sympathetic grin.

I laughed it off.

Because honestly?

It felt right.

A tiny, ridiculous moment of normality in the middle of the biggest day of my life.

I found my seat, placed my bag under the chair, and sat down.

The engines hummed.
 People settled in.
 The cabin lights dimmed slightly.

And as the plane began to taxi toward the runway, I felt it — that quiet, powerful shift inside me.

This wasn't just a flight.

This was the moment my life split into a before and an after.

The moment the world tilted toward everything I had been waiting for.

The moment the journey truly began.

I closed my eyes, breathed in, and let the truth settle into my chest:

I'm on my way to her.

CHAPTER NINETEEN

The Flight

The engines rumbled beneath me as the plane began to move, a low vibration that travelled up through the floor into my chest.

People around me were settling in — adjusting seats, opening snacks, scrolling through their phones — but I just sat there, staring ahead, feeling the weight of that moment.

This was it.

The point of no return.

The moment the world shifted from "one day" to "today."

As the plane lifted off the ground, my stomach dropped — not from fear, but from the overwhelming truth of what was happening.

I was leaving everything I had ever known behind.
 I was flying toward everything I had ever wanted.

The first hour passed in a blur.

I put on a movie — something I'd seen before — but I barely registered a single scene.

My mind kept drifting back to her.

To the first message.
 To the first call.
 To the nights we stayed awake until sunrise.
 To the years of distance, hope, frustration, and love.

Every mile the plane travelled felt like a thread pulling me closer to her.

Eventually, I turned toward the window.

And that was when the world opened up.

The clouds stretched out beneath me like an endless, white ocean.

The sun spilled across them in gold, turning everything soft and glowing.

It didn't look real — it looked like something from a dream, a place
between worlds.

I took photos.
 I took videos.

Not because I needed them, but because I wanted to remember how it felt
to see the world from above on the day my life changed.

Every time I looked out, I felt the same thing:

I'm getting closer to our little slice of heaven.
 And she's my angel waiting at the end of it.

Up there, suspended between two continents, it felt almost spiritual —
like the universe was carrying me toward her.

Every mile felt like a heartbeat.
Every cloud felt like a step closer.
Every moment felt like a whisper:

You're nearly there.
She's waiting.
Keep going.

Hours passed.
Time blurred.

The cabin lights dimmed and brightened in cycles that didn't match the
world outside.

I drifted in and out of sleep — the kind of half-sleep where your body
rests but your mind keeps moving.

Every time I opened my eyes, the sky looked different.

Sometimes dark.
Sometimes bright.
Sometimes painted in colours I'd never seen before.

It felt like travelling through time as much as space.

The layover hit me harder than I expected.

Standing in a different country, halfway across the world, I realised:

I'm closer to her than I've ever been.
I'm really doing this.
I'm going to see her today.

My hands shook.
My heart raced.

I felt like I was floating and sinking at the same time.

I messaged her.
She messaged back instantly.

Just seeing her name on my screen made everything inside me tighten with anticipation.

The second flight felt shorter, even though it wasn't.

Every minute felt like a countdown.
Every announcement felt like a step closer.
Every mile felt like a heartbeat.

The ring was in my bag, inches away from me.

A promise waiting to be spoken.
A future waiting to begin.

When the plane finally began to descend, the world outside the window looked different — brighter, warmer, alive.

The clouds parted.
The land appeared.
The sun hit the wing in a way that made it glow.

My chest tightened.

This was her world.
Her sky.
Her home.

The wheels touched down.
The plane slowed down.
The seatbelt sign dinged.

People stood up, reaching for their bags, stretching, talking.

But I just sat there for a moment, breathing, feeling my heart pounding in my chest.

Because she was here.

In the same country.
Breathing the same air.
Waiting for me.

I stood up, grabbed my bag, and stepped into the aisle.

The next steps I took would lead me to her.

And for the first time in my life,
I felt like I was walking into my future.

CHAPTER TWENTY

Arrival

The moment the plane door opened in Manila, the air hit me like a wave — warm, thick, humid, and alive.

It wrapped around me instantly, heavy but comforting, like the country itself was saying, 'Welcome. You made it.'

I stepped out of the jet bridge and felt something shift inside me.

A strange calm settled over me — the kind that only comes when your body knows you're exactly where you're meant to be.

The airport was chaotic — people everywhere, voices echoing, luggage wheels rattling, announcements blaring — but none of it touched me.

I moved through it with a kind of quiet focus, like I was walking through a dream.

Immigration was surprisingly smooth.

They asked why I was visiting.

"Pleasure," I said — and it was the truth in every sense.

They stamped my passport, handed it back, and just like that...

I was officially in the Philippines.

Her country.
Her world.
Her home.

And now, mine too — even if just for a while.

I collected my bags and headed outside, because Manila's terminals aren't connected.

You have to leave the building, find a taxi, and hope the driver understands where you need to go.

The heat outside was unreal — like stepping into a sauna, but with traffic.

Cars honking, people shouting, engines revving, the smell of exhaust mixed with street food drifting through the air.

It was overwhelming.
It was chaotic.
It was alive.

And underneath all of it was one steady thought:

I'm on her soil.
I'm getting closer.

The taxi ride between terminals was fast and frantic.

The driver wove through traffic like he was in a video game.

I held onto the seat in front of me, half-laughing, half-praying, but even then... I felt calm.

Nothing could shake me.
 Not today.

The domestic flight to Bacolod felt like nothing — a blink, a breath, a moment suspended in time.

I was exhausted, but adrenaline carried me through.

When the plane landed, something inside me tightened.

I'm on the right island.
 Negros Occidental.
 Maria's home.

Just a four-hour bus ride away.

The thought made my chest buzz with anticipation.

The hotel in Bacolod surprised me.

It was modern, clean, bright — far nicer than I expected.

The room smelled fresh, like new sheets and air-conditioning.

Outside the window, tricycles buzzed past like colourful insects, weaving through the night.

I took videos of everything — the room, the view, the lights outside — not to show off, but to tell her:

"I'm here.
I made it.
I'm in Bacolod."

She was so excited.

Her voice was soft, emotional, full of disbelief and joy.

Then I lay on the huge bed, phone plugged in, camera still on.

We watched each other fall asleep.

Every few seconds, one of us would open our eyes again, just to check the other was still there.

Neither of us wanted to miss a moment.

It was tender.
It was sweet.
It was emotional.

The last night before everything changed.

The morning of 15 August felt electric.

I woke up with a steady heart — not nervous, not scared, just ready.

I messaged her.
She messaged back instantly.

I dressed carefully, choosing clothes that felt right for the moment.

Not fancy.
 Not overdone.

Just me.

I checked out of the hotel, got a ride to the bus terminal, and climbed onto the bus — the final stretch of the journey.

The front seats were raised slightly, giving me a perfect view out the front window and the right side.

As we pulled away, something inside me shifted again.

Every mile was a heartbeat.
 Every turn was a step closer.
 Every moment was a countdown.

The Philippines felt warm, friendly, alive.

People smiled at me.
 People chatted.
 People lived with a kind of openness I wasn't used to.

The bus made a few stops along the way.

At the last one, my bags were moved farther back, so when I got back on, I sat halfway down the bus.

And then... the coastline appeared.

The ocean.
 Blue, endless, beautiful.

Nothing like the beaches back home.

This was paradise.

As we approached Sipalay, I saw the shops lining the road, the people walking, the life happening all around us.

Then I saw it:

The Sipalay sign.
 Right on the beach.

My heart started pounding.

The bus turned left into the huge open area where the buses swing around.

From my window, I could see a crowd gathered near the waiting area with benches.

I didn't see her.

But I knew she was there.

This was it.

Two and a half years of waiting.
 Two and a half years of distance.
 Two and a half years of longing.

All coming down to this moment.

The bus stopped.

People got off.
 One by one.

I was the last.

I stood up, grabbed my two bags, and walked slowly toward the front.

The driver reached out and took my heavy bag.

I kept the carry-on over my shoulder.

My heart was hammering.

I stepped down onto the ground.

The heat hit me.
 The noise.
 The crowd.
 The reality.

I stopped for a second, taking it all in.

A girl walked across my path to the right — not Maria.

My eyes followed her for a moment.

And then I heard it.

One word.

"Babe."

I turned.

And everything changed.

CHAPTER TWENTY-ONE

The Hug That Changed Everything

She was running toward me — tiny, fast, emotional — her whole body moving with a kind of desperate joy I had never seen before.

And then she collided with me.

Not a gentle hug.
Not a shy hug.

A full-force, arms-around-my-neck, shaking, sobbing, clinging hug that nearly knocked the breath out of my chest.

Her arms wrapped around me like she never wanted to let go.

Her face buried into my chest.
Her whole body trembled.

It was the hug we had talked about.
The hug we had waited for.

Two and a half years of hugs in one moment.

I held her.

I held her like I had been waiting my whole life to do it.

The crowd around us erupted — cheering, clapping, smiling.

A drone buzzed overhead, capturing it all.

No drama.
 No hesitation.

Just pure love.

She kept saying, "Don't leave. Don't leave."

"Why would I leave you?" I said.

She sobbed harder.

"I thought you'd see me and turn and get back on the bus."

I leaned down, trying to hear her through the tears.

"Where would I go?" I said softly.

"You're my guide. Without you, I'd be lost."

And it was true — not just in that moment, but in every moment since the night I messaged her on 2 October 2019.

I tried to get her to look at me.

"Babe... look at me. I'm here."

She finally lifted her head.

"I'm ugly," she said through tears.

"No," I told her.

"You're beautiful.
 Look at me... and kiss me.
 What happened to my kiss?"

She looked up.

And then it happened.

The kiss she thought she'd be too shy for.
 The kiss we had waited two and a half years for.

The moment her lips touched mine, the entire terminal disappeared.

The noise, the heat, the people — all of it dropped away like someone had turned down the volume on the world.

It was just us.

Finally us.

But the world didn't disappear for everyone else.

People around us gasped, cheered, clapped, laughed, even filmed.

But Maria didn't care.

She held onto me like none of them existed.

It lasted for minutes.

It was everything.

Want.
Need.
Desire.
Love.

All of it.

When we finally pulled apart, she hugged me again, wiping her tears.

Then I felt her body dip slightly — the heat, the emotion, the sun — all of it hitting her at once.

I held her tight.

"Let's sit," I said gently.

She didn't let go.

We just shuffled together towards the benches, still wrapped around each other.

The crowd was still clapping.
Still cheering.
Still smiling.

We sat in the shade, cooling off — from the sun and from everything else.

And in that moment, with her tiny body pressed against mine, her hand gripping my shirt, her head on my chest...

I knew:

My life had just changed forever.

When the crew finally guided us toward the van, we were still holding onto each other, still overwhelmed.

We climbed into the back seat together, forgetting completely that the microphones were still clipped to us.

Inside the van, the door closed, and for the first time since I arrived, it felt like we were alone.

We whispered, laughed softly, held hands — just the closeness of two people who had waited years for this moment.

At one point she buried her face in my arm again, shy and emotional, still trying to process everything.

I held her hand, letting her breathe, letting her settle.

The microphones picked up every quiet sound — every breath, every laugh, every whispered word — but we didn't know that yet.

We were just together.

Finally together.

CHAPTER TWENTY-TWO

Our Little Yellow House

When the cheering finally faded and the drone drifted away, Maria's hand found mine again — small, warm, trembling.

We weren't surrounded by a crowd anymore.

We weren't performing for cameras or strangers.

It was just us now, walking away from the noise and into the next part of our story.

She kept glancing up at me like she was afraid I might disappear if she blinked too long.

And I kept looking down at her, still trying to believe she was real — not pixels, not a voice through a speaker, not a dream I'd been holding onto for two and a half years.

We stepped out of the terminal area together.

And everything felt lighter.

A tricycle pulled up, the driver smiling like he already knew our whole story.

Maria grabbed my arm immediately, holding on like she was afraid I might vanish if she let go.

And then she started doing something that made my heart melt.

She kept lightly pinching me.

Not hard.
 Not playful.

Just these tiny, gentle pinches on my arm, over and over, like she was checking if I was real.

Her other hand was wrapped around mine, fingers laced, holding on like she'd waited two and a half years for this moment — because she had.

As we climbed into the tricycle, she didn't stop.

Pinch.
 Hold.
 Pinch.
 Hold.

I laughed softly and said, half-joking, half-serious:

"Babe... don't pinch me.
 I don't want this dream to end."

She just smiled, eyes shining, and pinched me again anyway.

Honestly?

I think she needed to feel me — to reassure herself that I wasn't a screen anymore.

I was warmth, presence, reality.

It was one of the sweetest moments of the entire day.

The tricycle buzzed through Sipalay, weaving past shops, houses, and people who had just watched our reunion.

Maria stayed glued to my side the whole way, her hand never leaving mine, her tiny fingers still giving those soft little pinches.

It was about 1 p.m., exactly as we'd planned.

Exactly as we had imagined.

We pulled up outside her aunt's little yellow house — the place we had rented so we could finally be alone together.

Maria led me inside with this shy, excited pride that melted me completely.

She gave me a quick tour — the bedroom, the little kitchen, the bathroom, the living area.

It was simple, warm, colourful, and perfect.

It was ours.

A place where we could finally be a couple in the real world.

A place where we could finally close a door and just... be.

I dropped my bags, still buzzing from everything that had just happened, and before I could even settle, Maria said:

"Come. We will go to my parents."

And suddenly the nerves hit me harder than anything that day.

Meeting Maria?

That I understood.

That I had imagined a thousand times.

That was love — the real kind.

Meeting her family?

That was something else entirely.

We crossed the road to her parents' house, and I felt my stomach twist.

Maria was quiet — quieter than I had ever seen her — and I realised she was nervous too.

Her sister stepped in immediately, smiling, ready to translate.

Thank God for her.

She was brilliant — calm, friendly, patient.

I greeted her parents, trying to be respectful, trying to show them I was genuine, trying not to look like a giant foreigner who'd just landed to steal their daughter away.

They looked... surprised.

Not in a bad way — more like they didn't quite know what to make of the situation.

Maybe they expected me to take Maria away immediately.

Maybe they didn't expect the cameras.

Maybe they didn't expect the emotion.

It was awkward.
 Stiff.
 Strange.

Maria barely spoke — too shy, too overwhelmed — so I relied on her sister to help me communicate.

We exchanged a few words, a few smiles, a few polite nods.

But it wasn't flowing.
 Not yet.

And Maria must have sensed it, because she gently took my hand and said:

"Come. I show you the beach."

We walked just a few steps down the road, and suddenly the world opened up.

The beach.
 The ocean.
 Paradise.

The view was breathtaking — the kind of beauty that doesn't feel real until you're standing in it.

And out on the water, rising from the sea like a dream, was Danjugan Island.

Maria pointed to it.

"I see it every day," she said softly.
 "But I've never been there."

I didn't know it then, but that island would become one of the most important places of our entire trip.

As we stood there, taking in the view, I became aware of something behind us.

People.
 Neighbours.
 Locals.
 Kids.

All watching us.

The children were the funniest — running behind us, giggling, whispering, staring at the tall foreigner and the tiny Filipina holding his hand.

And when we kissed — just a small kiss — and the giggling exploded.

I felt like a movie star.

Not because of ego, but because the moment felt unreal, like something out of a film.

Two people who had waited years finally standing together on a beach in paradise, surrounded by curious eyes and warm smiles.

After the filming wrapped, the crew finally lowered their cameras and unclipped the microphones.

The whole atmosphere shifted instantly.

One of the crew members gave us a small, warm, knowing smile.

"OK, you two. I know you two love birds want to be alone. Go ahead and enjoy your night — and we'll see you in the morning."

I don't think Maria even heard him.

She was too shy, too overwhelmed, too caught up in everything that had happened.

But I heard him clearly — and I couldn't help it.

I had the biggest smile.

It wasn't embarrassing.

It was the feeling of being seen, understood, and quietly approved of.

Maria hid her face in my arm, still not realising what he'd said, just reacting to the attention.

I laughed softly, because I knew exactly what the crew meant.

They let us walk away alone.

No cameras.
 No microphones.
 No instructions.

Just the two of us walking through her neighbourhood as the sky turned orange, heading toward the little yellow house that would become our first home together.

By the time we walked back to the yellow house, it was around 5 p.m.

In the Philippines, the sun drops fast — one moment bright, the next moment dusk.

We stepped inside, closed the door...

And everything changed.

The world outside faded.

The noise, the heat, the crowd, the nerves — all gone.

It was just us.

For the first time ever, we were alone together.

No screens.
No distance.
No time zones.
No waiting.

Just two people who had loved each other for two and a half years finally sharing the same space.

We kissed.
We held each other.
We laughed.
We breathed.

We existed together, naturally, effortlessly, like we'd lived together for years.

It felt right.
It felt easy.
It felt like home.

That night, in our little yellow house, we weren't visitors or strangers or long-distance lovers.

We were a couple.

A real couple.

Living together for the first time.

And it felt exactly the way I always knew it would.

CHAPTER TWENTY-THREE

Our First Morning Together

The first morning in the little yellow house didn't feel like waking up in a new place.

It felt like waking up in a life that had been waiting for us, paused, just out of reach, until we finally arrived.

I opened my eyes to the sound of roosters — the same roosters I had heard through Maria's phone for months whenever she was back in the Philippines.

But this time, they weren't coming through a speaker.

They were outside our window, mixed with the low hum of tricycles starting their day and the soft chatter of neighbours already awake.

The room was washed in that warm, early Filipino light — pale gold, already hinting at the heat that was coming.

The fan hummed in the corner, pushing warm air around but not really cooling anything.

I could smell the faint scent of Maria's shampoo on the pillow beside me.

And her breath was warm against my chest, her tiny body curled into mine like she had always slept there.

For a moment, I didn't move.

I just let the truth settle in.

She's here.
She's real.
I'm waking up beside her.

After two and a half years of falling asleep miles apart, holding phones
instead of each other, this felt surreal — peaceful and overwhelming at the
same time.

We had barely slept.
 The heat was heavy, sticky, the kind that clings to your skin and makes the
night feel endless.
 But we weren't really trying to sleep anyway.
 We were making up for every night we had spent alone.

Every time she drifted a few inches away in her sleep, I pulled her back.
 Every time I shifted, she reached for me without even waking.
 It was instinctive, natural, like our bodies were trying to catch up on years
of distance in a single night.

When she finally opened her eyes, she didn't say anything.
 She just smiled — sleepy, soft, glowing — then got up and slipped on the
T-shirt I'd been wearing when we met at the bus station the day before.

She didn't do it shyly.
 She didn't do it playfully.
 She did it like it was the most natural thing in the world.
 Like of course she would wear my shirt now.
 Of course she would smell like me.
 Of course we belonged to each other.

We were still wrapped around each other, teasing quietly, when we heard footsteps outside.

The crew had arrived earlier than expected.

We weren't ready.
We hadn't showered.
We were still in that private bubble where the world didn't exist.
But we had to get up.

Maria showered first, switching into her usual T-shirt and cute shorts — the outfit I'd seen her wear a thousand times on video calls.
Seeing her in it, in real life, in our house, made everything feel even more real.
This was the girl I had fallen in love with.
Not the Albert station version.
Not the camera version.
Just her.

I showered after her, trying to cool down from the heat outside, but the moment I stepped out, the humidity wrapped around me again.
It was going to be one of those days—hot, sticky, relentless.
But I didn't care.
I was exactly where I wanted to be.

We stepped out onto the porch for breakfast.
The patio was simple but beautiful — open, shaded, with a table and chairs that looked out onto the road.
It felt like the heart of the house, the place where mornings were meant to begin.

We walked to the sari-sari store hand in hand, still glued to each other like magnets.
We bought bread, fruit, snacks and milk.
Hot milk — something I never drank at home, but something that became our morning ritual instantly.

We sat side by side on the porch, eating quietly, watching the world pass by.
The heat was already rising off the road, shimmering in the sunlight.
Tricycles buzzed past in a steady rhythm.
Kids ran along the street.
Neighbours greeted each other.
The air smelled like dust, morning sun, and the faint sweetness of fruit from the store.

Every single person who passed looked at me.
I stuck out like a sore thumb—a six-foot-three white guy in the middle of a small Philippine province.
People slowed down.
Some stared.
Some smiled.
Some whispered.

Maria squeezed my hand every time someone looked.
She was smiling, proud, almost glowing.

And honestly, I enjoyed the attention.
Not because of ego, but because it felt like the world could finally see what we had been fighting for.

Sitting there with her, drinking hot milk in the morning heat, watching tricycles and neighbours and the bright sun rising over the road, I felt something settle inside me.

It felt like home.

Not because of the house.
Not because of the place.
But because she was there.
Because we were finally together.
Because after everything — the distance, the waiting, the calls, the nights alone — we were exactly where we were supposed to be.

It felt like the world had stood still just long enough for us to step into the life we were meant to have.

It was peaceful.
Overwhelming.
Surreal.

Our first morning together wasn't dramatic or loud—it didn't need to be.
It wasn't a big moment.

It was simple.
Quiet.
Warm.
Real.

And that's what made it perfect.

CHAPTER TWENTY-FOUR

Sipalay Market, Pearl Beach & The First Proposal

It was the kind of morning that felt ordinary to everyone else...
 but extraordinary to us.

Because it was our first full day together.

But we didn't stay local.
 "Come, babe," Maria said.
 "We go to Sipalay market."

We didn't waste time—the day felt too full of possibility.
 So we climbed into a tricycle and headed back up the coast, the same road
we had travelled the day before—but now as a couple, not strangers
meeting for the first time.
 The difference was everything.

The Sipalay market was a world of its own.
 Crowded.
 Colourful.
 Chaotic.
 Alive.
 And absolutely not designed for tall people.

I ducked under low beams and tarpaulin roofs while Maria laughed,
holding my hand and guiding me through the maze of stalls.
 People stared — even more than usual — but she stayed glued to my side,

proud and protective.
 She kept glancing up at me with this little smile, like she still couldn't believe I was real.

We bought food, snacks, drinks — everything we needed for later.
 Maria chose things she planned to grill for our sunset picnic.
 She was excited, focused, almost glowing at the idea of cooking for us on the beach.

It was one of those moments where I saw her future self — the woman who would run a home, cook for her family, build a life with me.
 Not because she had to, but because she wanted to.

When we finished, we headed back to Hinobigon.
 And for the first time that day, we slowed down.
 We put the market bags away, rested for a while and let the heat of the afternoon settle around us.
 The fan buzzed softly, the house felt calm, and we lay together talking, laughing, just enjoying the feeling of finally sharing a home.

The afternoon heat settled over Hinobigon, slowing everything down just enough for us to breathe before the evening began.
 It felt like a real home.
 Our home.

Later, when the sun began to dip lower in the sky, Maria grabbed the bags of food and smiled at me.
 "Come, babe... we go to Pearl Beach."

Pearl Beach in Bulata was only a short walk from the house, but it felt like another world.

Quiet.
Soft.
Golden.
The kind of place where the sunset looks like it's been painted just for you.

We found a spot on the sand, close enough to hear the waves, but far enough from the few people around.
 Maria opened the bags and began preparing everything right there —
cutting the fruit on a small board, arranging it neatly, then setting up the grill.
 The smell of the sea mixed with the smoke from the charcoal.

She stood over the grill, carefully turning the meat, the orange glow of the fire lighting her face.
 Every few minutes, she looked back at me with that shy, excited smile —
proud to be cooking for us, proud to be sharing this moment.

It was simple.
 It was intimate.
 It was ours.

We sat together on the sand, eating, talking, watching the sun melt into the horizon.

And then the conversation shifted.

I said to her, quietly, honestly:
 "I know we always said you'd come to the UK eventually…
 but is it possible for me to stay here?
 Long-term?"

I knew the answer.
 But I needed to ask.

She looked at me with so much love — and so much realism.
 She explained gently:

I wouldn't be able to get work there,
 Even if I did, the wages wouldn't be enough,
 Even both of us working 12 hours a day wouldn't cover a proper life,
 I wouldn't learn the language,
 I wouldn't have opportunities,

And from the very beginning, she had always been ready to come to the UK.

She said it softly, but with certainty:
 "It's better I come to you.
 I'm ready for that."

It wasn't a sad conversation.
 It was honest.
 It was practical.
 It was two people planning a future that suddenly felt real.

The conversation stayed with me as we walked home that evening, settling somewhere deep, mixing with the heat and the sound of the waves still echoing in my head.

Later that night, after we had settled into bed, the room was quiet and warm, something shifted inside me.

I had slept with the ring under my pillow the night before — a secret I'd kept close to my heart.

And in that moment, lying beside her, feeling the weight of everything we had shared that day, I reached under the pillow and closed my hand around it.

I hadn't planned it.
I hadn't rehearsed it.
It wasn't dramatic or staged.

It was just... right.

I sat up slightly, looked at her, and before I could overthink it, I opened the box.

Maria's breath caught.
Her eyes widened.
Her hand flew to her mouth.
Her whole body froze.

Her yes came instantly—soft but full of excitement, full of love, full of everything we had been waiting for.

But behind her eyes, just for a moment, something flickered.
Not hesitation.
Not doubt.
Not fear.

Something cultural.
 Something respectful.
 Something she had been raised to honour.

And in that split second, it hit me — a sudden punch of awareness.

I hadn't asked her father.
 I hadn't done it the right way.

I hadn't meant to disrespect anyone — but intention didn't matter.
 What mattered was fixing it.

She didn't say anything — not then — but I felt it.
 She felt it.

The moment was beautiful, but it was incomplete.

We fell asleep holding each other, but I knew what I had to do.

CHAPTER TWENTY-FIVE

The Awkward Day, The Announcement & The Midnight Meeting

The morning after the proposal felt different.
Not bad.
Not broken.
Just... heavier.

We woke up in the little yellow house in Hinobigon the same way we had the day before — tangled together, clinging to each other like the night wasn't long enough.
But beneath the warmth, beneath the closeness, there was a quiet tension neither of us wanted to name.

I had proposed.
She had said yes.
But I hadn't asked her father.

And in the Philippines, that wasn't a small thing.

It was tradition.
Respect.
Family.

Maria didn't say anything, but I could feel it in the way she held me — still loving, still close, but thoughtful.
 And I felt it in myself too.

A knot in my stomach.
 A whisper in my mind:

You rushed it.
 You need to fix this.

We tried to keep the day normal, so in the morning we went for a short hike to a high point overlooking the surrounding mountains.

The view was beautiful — layers of green stretching out in every direction — but the weather was turning bad.
 Dark clouds rolled in fast, the wind picking up, the air shifting.

We didn't stay long.
 Just a few minutes taking in the scenery before heading back home, both of us pretending everything was fine, even though the weight of the night before still lingered quietly between us.

Later that afternoon, we went to her sister's farewell party.
 She would soon be working away, and the family wanted to celebrate her before she left.

The moment we arrived, the place was already alive — music blasting, people everywhere, kids running around, laughter spilling out of the house.

The smell of grilled pork drifted through the air, mixing with the sound of videoke and the chatter of relatives calling out greetings.

Before I even had time to settle, someone handed me a machete.
 Not a small knife — a proper Filipino bolo.

They pointed to the banana trees and told me to get the leaves for the boodle fight.

So there I was, hacking huge banana leaves straight from the tree, trying to look like I knew what I was doing while everyone laughed and shouted instructions at me.

Maria and her family handled the tuna and the cooking, moving around each other with the kind of rhythm only families have.

I carried the leaves back, wiped them down, and laid them out the way they showed me.
 It felt good to be part of it — not just watching, but actually helping.

When the food was ready, everything was laid out on the banana leaves.
 No plates.
 No cutlery.
 Just hands, laughter, and food shared the Filipino way.

Maria even grabbed the microphone and sang a song on videoke, smiling at me between lines like she couldn't believe I was actually there, helping her family.

For a moment, everything felt light.

But beneath it all, something else remained.

A question.
A missing step.
A tradition not followed.

At some point — I don't even remember who spoke first — we announced it:

We were engaged.

There were smiles.
There were congratulations.
There were surprised looks.
There were curious glances from relatives.

But behind it all, there was that unspoken thing everyone felt but no one said.

Maria's sister translated for us, helping bridge the gap between cultures, expectations, and what I had done versus what I should have done.

Her family wasn't unkind.
They weren't cold.
They weren't angry.

But they were... surprised.

And Maria, standing beside me, knew exactly why.

She didn't scold me.
She didn't blame me.
She didn't make me feel small.

She simply held my hand and stayed close — but her eyes told me the truth:

This wasn't the proper way.

We left the party just after nightfall, walking back to the yellow house.

The air was warm, the village quieting down, the sky darkening into a soft, star-scattered blue.

Back home, we rested, talked a little, and ate again closer to midnight — leftovers from the boodle fight, still tasting of charcoal and salt.

Hours passed — three, maybe four — before Maria remembered we needed to take food back to her parents' house.

So we went out again.

We crossed the road and stepped onto the narrow single-slab path between two rice fields, the moonlight reflecting off the water.

The whole village was silent except for crickets and the occasional dog barking in the distance.

When we reached the edge near her family's home, I stopped.

"I'll wait here," I told her.

She nodded and went inside with the food.

I stood there alone, just out of sight, the night warm and still.

And then something unexpected happened.

Her father came out.

He saw me standing there at the edge of the path, and without hesitation, he gestured for me to come.

Not angry.
 Not confused.
 Just... welcoming.

I walked toward him, nervous but determined.

When I reached him, I tried to do a respectful gesture — taking his hand and placing it on my forehead.

But he didn't let me.

He grabbed my hand, shook it firmly, and gently pulled me toward the house.

No hesitation.
 No coldness.
 Just warmth.

He sat me down outside at the table, smiling, relaxed, as if he had been waiting for me.

But we couldn't communicate.
 Not properly — not really at all.

And then — like fate — Maria's sister appeared.

My saviour.

She sat with us, and I told her quietly:

"I need to talk to him — can you help me again?"

She nodded.

So I told her everything.

I told her I knew I had messed up by proposing without speaking to him
first.
 I told her the moment had overwhelmed me.
 I told her we had been together for two and a half years, and when I
looked at Maria that night, I just acted.

I apologised.
 Sincerely,
 From the heart.

She translated every word.

Her father listened.
 Slowly.
 Thoughtfully.

Then he spoke.

And her sister translated:

"He understands.
 He did the same when he was young."

She went on to explain what happened back then — how he proposed without asking permission first, how he followed his heart just like I did.

He laughed softly as she said it — a warm, genuine laugh that dissolved every bit of tension in the room.

Suddenly the air felt clear.

Clearer than it had since the moment I proposed.

We all laughed together — me, her father, her sister — sitting in that small house, surrounded by warmth and acceptance.

He grabbed my hand again, and in that moment, I knew everything was okay.

But I also knew something else:

I would have to do this again tomorrow.
On camera.
For the show.

The film crew had no idea I was there.
This conversation wasn't planned.
It wasn't staged.
It wasn't part of the schedule.

But it was real.
Honest.

It was the moment that truly fixed everything.

When Maria finally came out of the house, she didn't know the details yet — but she could see the ease in my face, the comfort in her father's.

We walked back across the rice fields together, the night warm around us, the path lit only by the moon and the soft glow of distant houses.

Back at the yellow house, we settled in for the night.

And for the first time since the proposal, I felt light again.

I had made it right.

Tomorrow, I would do it the proper way — the way her culture deserved, the way her family expected, the way she would be proud of.

But tonight?

Tonight, I had already earned her father's trust — and that meant everything.

CHAPTER TWENTY-SIX

The Blessing & The Journey to Danjugan Island

The morning of 18 August began with purpose.
Not nerves.
Not fear.
Not uncertainty.
Purpose.

The air was already warm — the kind of heat that settles on your skin
before the day had even begun — this was the morning everything needed
to be put right.
Properly.
Respectfully.
On camera — with the blessing that mattered most.

Maria and I walked together across the narrow single-slab path between
the rice fields, the same path we crossed the night before.
But this time, the film crew followed behind us, capturing every step,
every breath, every subtle shift in the air.

The rice fields shimmered in the morning light, the water reflecting the
sky like glass.
The humidity clung to us, thick and heavy, but inside me, something felt
calm.

I knew what I had to do.

When we reached her family's house, I turned to Maria and said:

"Babe... I just need to talk to your sister for a second — you go ahead and wait for the boat."

She nodded, trusting me completely, and walked toward the beach to wait for the small boat that would take us to Danjugan Island.

I stayed behind.

This was my moment.

Outside the house, her father was waiting.
Calm.
Warm.
Exactly as he had been the night before.

Maria's sister stood beside him — my bridge, my translator, my lifeline.
This part was mine.

I took a breath.

"I apologised last night," I told her, "but I didn't ask him the important part. I saved that for today."

She nodded and translated.

Her father listened, patient and steady, his eyes soft, his posture relaxed.

Then I said the words that mattered:

"I love Maria. I want to marry her. I want to do this the right way. I'm asking for your permission."

He smiled — the same gentle smile from the night before — and spoke softly.

Maria's sister translated:

"He says... if you are the same. If you treat Maria the way her family treats her... then yes. It's okay."

He gave his blessing.
 He shook my hand.

And in that moment, something inside me lifted — the shy lad from Warrington who had flown 7,000 miles for a girl suddenly felt like he belonged. Like he had earned his place. Like everything was finally as it should be.

We laughed together — me, her father, her sister — and the air felt light, clean, right.

Now it was time.

Time to go to the beach.
 Time to meet Maria.
 Time to begin the day that would change everything.

When I reached the beach, the sky shifted.

One minute it was boiling hot — the kind of heat that sticks to your skin.
The next, the heavens opened.

Rain. Heavy, tropical, drenching rain.

We stood there laughing, soaked, waiting for the boat, which took another ten or fifteen minutes to arrive.
It was ridiculous and perfect at the same time — the kind of moment you never forget for the rest of your life.

Maria kept wiping the water from her face, laughing like a child, her hair plastered to her cheeks.
I couldn't stop smiling.
Even the film crew were laughing behind their cameras.

And then, just as suddenly as it started, the rain stopped.
The heat returned.
The world felt beautiful again.

The boat arrived.

We climbed in.

And as we pulled away from the shore, I felt it — I knew exactly what the day would bring.

Danjugan Island rose out of the water like something from a dream — untouched, wild, impossibly beautiful.

The water around it was turquoise, almost glowing.
The trees were thick and green, the air filled with the smell of salt and

warm earth.
It felt like stepping into a postcard — another world entirely.

We met our guide, who would take us around the island.
First the tour.
Then the snorkeling.
Then the magic.

He led us into the forest, the heat thick under the trees, the sound buzzing all around us.

The walk to the bat cave was longer than I expected — a proper trek through the greenery.
At one point we crossed a narrow bamboo bridge, just wide enough for one person at a time to cross.
Beneath it, the water was so clear you could see every fish as if they were floating in air, bright and sharp in the sunlight.

It didn't feel like a tourist spot.
It felt untouched, wild, real.

Eventually, we reached the bat cave.
The air inside was cool and damp, the sound of wings echoing above us.
The guide told us the story of a giant python that hunts there every day.

It was equal parts terrifying and fascinating — and Maria clung to me the whole time, gripping my arm like the snake might suddenly appear behind us.

Then we returned to the beach.

While the guide prepared the snorkeling gear, Maria and I wandered to a small cliff-edge lookout — a bamboo platform with a hammock hanging over the sea.

We sat together, the view stretching endlessly before us — turquoise water, white sand, the whole world seemed to glow.

The wind was warm.
The waves were soft.
The moment felt suspended — frozen in time.

I didn't know it then, but that spot would become the centrepiece of the night.

Then came the snorkeling.

We held onto the rubber ring as the guide pulled us through the crystal-clear water.
Fish darted beneath us.
Coral glowed in the sunlight.
And then — the turtles.

Massive, ancient, graceful.

It felt like floating through another world.

There was only one problem.

My mask kept leaking.

Apparently, I've got a funny-shaped face.

Maria laughed every time I had to stop and fix it — and I laughed too, even though it was annoying as hell.

We even had an underwater kiss — clumsy, hilarious, perfect.

And somewhere in all of it, I remember thinking this:

This is the girl I'm going to marry.

As the sun began to set, we swam together, kayaked, splashed each other, acted like kids.
 It was one of those rare days where everything feels light and free.

But the best part was still waiting.

The part that would change everything — the moment that would turn Danjugan Island into the place where our story shifted forever.

CHAPTER TWENTY-SEVEN

The Real Proposal

As the last light of the day faded over Danjugan Island, the world softened into gold. The air was warm, the sea calm, and everything felt suspended — like time itself was holding its breath for us.

Maria and I walked back to the beach after swimming and kayaking, still laughing, glowing from the day. Salt clung to our skin, our hair was messy from the water, and our smiles felt permanent. We had no idea what was waiting for us.

The guide told us to get changed for dinner, so we went back to our little hut. The geckos chattered from the walls, the waves whispered outside, and the whole island felt alive — like it knew what was about to happen.

When we returned to the cliff-edge lookout — the same bamboo platform where we had sat earlier in the hammock — everything had changed.

The hammock was gone.

In its place was a small table set for two. Candles flickered in the warm breeze. Soft lights hung from the trees above us. The ocean stretched out beneath us, glowing with the last traces of dusk.

Maria stopped walking.

Her breath caught.

Her eyes widened.

She looked at me, then at the table, then back at me — completely surprised, completely overwhelmed.

It was perfect.

Exactly the way it was meant to be.

We sat down together, the candles lighting her face, the sea behind her, the night settling around us like a blessing.

I took her hand.

"Babe," I said softly, "I talked to your father this morning."

Her eyes filled instantly — not with fear, but with something deeper. She knew how important that was. She knew what it meant.

"I wanted to make things right," I continued. "I wanted to do this properly. I have his blessing."

Her lips trembled. Her eyes glistened. Her whole body softened.

Then I said the words that would change everything:

"I just need to take the ring back."

I reached for her hand.

She didn't pull away. She didn't question it. She just watched me —
trusting me completely — as I slid the ring from her finger.

The world went quiet.

Just the sea.

Just the candles.

Just us.

I stood up, walked around her chair, and knelt beside her.

My heart was pounding.

My hands were shaking.

But my voice was steady.

"Maria... I have loved you for two and a half years. And I want to love you
for the rest of my life. You're the girl I want to spend my life with. Maria...
will you marry me?"

Her tears fell instantly — not from shock this time, but from relief —
from joy — from everything settling into place.

She nodded, crying, smiling, shaking.

"Yes," she whispered. "Yes... I'll marry you."

I slipped the ring back onto her finger — properly, this time. With her
father's blessing. With the right moment. With the right words. With the
right heart.

We hugged. We cried. We held each other like the world had finally aligned.

It was perfect.

Our perfect moment.

We ate dinner together under the lights, laughing, emotional, unable to stop looking at each other like it still wasn't real. The mosquitoes tried to eat me alive — another one of those small, unforgettable moments — so we took some food back to our hut.

We sat on the hammock outside, finishing our meal, talking about everything and nothing. The night was warm, the waves gentle, the island quiet except for the geckos chirping like they were laughing with us.

Then the magic happened.

As we lay back in the hammock, the darkness around us began to glow. Fireflies drifted through the trees, blinking softly, floating like tiny stars that had drifted down to earth just for us. They moved slowly, lighting up the night in warm pulses, surrounding us in a quiet, living constellation.

We didn't speak.

We didn't need to.

We just watched them, wrapped around each other, letting the moment sink in — the proposal, the blessing, the island, the fireflies dancing like the world was celebrating with us.

Eventually we went inside, giggling like teenagers, still buzzing from the moment, still unable to believe how perfect it had been.

We fell asleep wrapped around each other, the ring shining on her hand, the night full of promise.

Tomorrow would bring the goodbye we didn't want.

But tonight?

Tonight was ours.

CHAPTER TWENTY-EIGHT

The Last Morning, The Goodbye & The Journey Home

The morning after the perfect night on Danjugan Island felt unreal — like waking up inside a dream you weren't ready to leave.

The air was warm, the sea calm, and the world was quiet in that soft, golden way only islands seem to understand.

We sat together on the beach outside our little hut, the sand cool beneath us, the waves brushing the shore like a quiet lullaby.

I gave Maria all the gifts I had brought for her — things I had carried 7,000 miles, things I had imagined giving her for so long.

She opened them slowly, carefully, like each one was fragile.

She smiled, emotional, holding every item as if it carried a piece of my heart — which, in a way, it did.

The morning light caught her face, and for a moment it felt like time had stopped just for us.

But time was already moving faster than either of us could hold onto.

We packed our things.

We walked to the shore.

We waited for the boat that would take us back to her island — back to reality.

The ride across the water felt heavier than the ride there.

The sea was calm, but inside us everything churned.

We held hands the whole way, neither of us speaking much.

There was nothing left to say that we hadn't already said in a hundred different ways.

Everything had already been said in the way we held each other, the way we breathed together, the way we existed in those last quiet moments.

When we reached her island, her family was waiting.

This time, everything felt right.

Everything felt complete.

We told them — officially — that we were engaged.

Properly engaged.

With her father's blessing.

With the right moment.

With the right words.

Everyone was happy.

Everyone smiled.

Everyone hugged us.

And for a moment, I felt like I belonged there — like I was part of something bigger than myself, something rooted, warm, and real.

But the clock was ticking.

We said our goodbyes to her family, and then we walked back to the little yellow house in Hinobigon to pack my things.

I had one hour left.

Just one.

We made food, but neither of us touched it.

We just sat there, quiet, holding onto the last moments we had.

The fan hummed softly.

The heat pressed against the walls.

The world outside kept moving, but inside that little house, time felt frozen.

Four days... after years of planning a thirty-day trip.

Four days after waiting two and a half years to meet.

It wasn't enough.

It would never be enough.

When the tricycle arrived, Maria froze.

She had decided not to come with me to the Sipalay bus terminal — she said it would be too hard.

She kept some of my shirts, including the one I wore the first day I arrived.

A small piece of me she could hold onto when I wasn't there.

We hugged outside the yellow house.

She told me to go before she cried too much.

I got into the tricycle.

The driver began to pull away.

And then—

"Babe!"

I turned.

Maria was running toward me.

I shouted for the driver to stop.

We reached for each other, hands outstretched, and when she reached me, we embraced one more time — tight, desperate, unforgettable.

We kissed.

She whispered, "Go... before I can't let you."

And then she stepped back.

The driver pulled away.

I watched her run back inside the little yellow house, her shoulders shaking, her heart breaking — and I felt mine go with her.

Four days was never enough.

The ride to the Sipalay bus depot felt endless.

The world outside the window blurred — palm trees, tricycles, rice fields, shops — all passing by like a film I wasn't really watching.

Five hours on the bus felt even longer.

I checked into a small hotel, exhausted, emotional, and Maria cried on the phone until she couldn't speak anymore.

We slept apart for the first time since meeting.

It felt wrong.

Empty.

Colder than it should have been.

The next morning, I took the short flight to Manila.

Then the long flight home.

This time, I wasn't flying to Manchester.

I was flying to London.

As the plane circled overhead, I looked down at the city — the landmarks, the lights, the places people dream of visiting.

And I thought:

One day, I'll bring Maria here.

One day, she'll see this with me.

One day, she'll be there with me.

Home.

The plane touched down.

The trip was over.

But the story wasn't over.

Not even close.

EPILOGUE

The Beginning After the Beginning

When I landed back in London, the world felt familiar and completely changed at the same time.

The airport was the same — the long corridors, the echo of footsteps, the distant hum of announcements drifting through the air.
 The cold hit the same too — sharp, grey, biting in that way only the UK can be after weeks of tropical heat.
 Even the walk to baggage claim felt familiar: fluorescent lights, tired faces, the shuffle of travellers returning to their ordinary lives.

But I wasn't the same.

I had left the UK as a man who hoped.
 I returned as a man who believed.

Believed in love.
 Believed in himself.
 Believed in a future that no longer felt imagined, but real — something solid, something possible — something worth fighting for.

Seven thousand miles away, on a small island in the Philippines, the woman I loved was waking up without me.

Her shirts still smelled like me.
My shirts still smelled like her.
And somewhere in that little yellow house, the ring I had placed on her finger was catching the morning light.

We were engaged.

Properly.
With her father's blessing.
With the right moment, the right words, and the right heart.

But we were also apart again.

The distance hadn't disappeared — not yet.
The time zones still stretched between us.
The screens still separated our days and nights.
The ache of missing her returned the moment I stepped off the plane.

But something had changed.

The distance no longer felt like a wall.
It felt like a path — one we were already walking together, step by step, message by message, call by call.

Every message now carried a different weight.
Every call felt like a promise.
Every plan for the future felt like something we could reach if we just kept going.

I didn't know how long it would take.
 I didn't know what obstacles were waiting.
 I didn't know how many more flights, forms, or goodbyes we'd have to face.

But I knew this:

We were no longer nevermets.
 And we would never be apart forever.

The story of how we met, how we loved, how we fought for each other —
that was only the first chapter of our life.

The next chapter was already waiting.

A life together.
 A home together.
 A future built from everything we had survived to reach this point.

And as I stepped out of the airport into the cold London air, I realised
something simple and true:

This wasn't the end.
 This was the beginning after the beginning.

Because this time... I wasn't walking away from her.
 I was walking toward the life we were about to build together.

AUTHOR BIO

Matthew Warburton is a British writer whose life changed the moment a message from a woman 7,000 miles away appeared on his screen. What began as an ordinary day in an ordinary life became the start of an extraordinary journey — one defined by long-distance love, cultural discovery, heartbreak, hope, and the quiet courage required to keep choosing someone you could not touch.

His story was featured on Channel 4's *Nevermets*, where viewers followed his long-distance relationship with Maria and the challenges of love across continents. Through years of separation, missed moments, and the relentless pull of two different worlds, Matthew discovered not only the woman he would one day marry, but a deeper understanding of himself.

His writing is grounded in honesty and vulnerability, shaped by the belief that real stories — the imperfect ones, the painful ones, the ones that demand patience and faith — are the stories worth telling. He writes the way he lived it: truthfully, emotionally, and without embellishment. Every chapter reflects the moments that shaped him, the battles he fought, and the love that transformed his world.

Matthew now lives in the United Kingdom with his wife, Maria, continuing the story they fought so hard to begin — a story that carries on long after the final page.

WHAT COMES NEXT

The story didn't end when the plane landed in London.
It only changed shape.

Ahead of us were new challenges — harder, heavier, and more complicated than distance alone:
Immigration.
Paperwork.
Interviews.
Uncertainty.
Months of waiting.
Nights of fear.
Days of hope.

But there were victories too.
Moments of joy.
Steps forward.
Miracles we never expected.

Book Two continues the journey — the fight to build a life together, the battles we never saw coming, and the love that carried us through the darkest moments.

If Book One, *Oceans Apart*, shared our story with readers — and reached audiences on Channel 4's *Nevermets* —
 Book Two is the story of how we held on, how far we were willing to go, and how two worlds finally became one.

This is the continuation of the story we began — a story about love, resilience, and the extraordinary ordinary moments that define a life together.

CONNECT ONLINE

Follow our journey and connect with us:

Facebook: Maria Warburton
YouTube: MattAndMariaVlog
TikTok: @MattAndMariaWarburton

CREDITS

Cover Photo: Maria Gajo

Cover Design: Matthew Warburton

Edited by: the author

Published by: Mattandmariavlog

Book Layout and Preparation: Matthew Warburton

All content © Matthew Warburton